MW01532452

The Delaware & Northern
and the Towns It Served

The Delaware & Northern

and the Towns It Served

by
Gertrude Fitch Horton

PURPLE MOUNTAIN PRESS
Fleischmanns, New York

First Edition
1989

Copyright © 1989 Gertrude Fitch Horton

Published by Purple Mountain Press, Ltd.
Main Street, P.O. Box E-3
Fleischmanns, New York 12430
914-254-4062

All rights reserved. No part of this publication may be reproduced or transmitted in any form without permission in writing from the publisher, except by a reviewer who wishes to quote brief passages in connection with a review written for inclusion in a magazine, newspaper or broadcast.

On the cover: D&N Engine #10 at Margaretville, May 30, 1938.
From the collection of L&L Photos.

Frontispiece: Engine #10 with a freight train.
From the collection of Edward P. Baumgardner.

ISBN (paperback) 0-935796-14-2

ISBN (hardcover) 0-935796-15-0

Printed in the USA

ACKNOWLEDGMENTS

My son, Stanley Horton, was a railroad buff. He collected memorabilia from many railroads, but his first interest was in the Delaware & Northern Railroad. He planned to write a book someday, but died before he could write it. A lot of the papers and pictures in this book are from his personal scrap book. He was my inspiration for this book.

The book is also in memory of my father, Roma Fitch, who was an engineer on the D&N until his death in 1933. I heard stories of what was happening on this road during all the years I was growing up. The talk around the table as we ate our evening meal was all about my father's day on the railroad. My father even allowed me to "drive" both the steam engines and the Brill Car. I have many fond memories of those years.

I am including in the book many old pictures of the towns once served by the D&N, as I believe they will be of much interest to the present inhabitants of the area. Some pictures are of communities which were destroyed by the Pepacton Reservoir built by New York City.

I have had a lot of help with this book, for which I am very grateful. My sister, Marjorie Fitch, and Merlin Twaddell both loaned me many old post cards, and Marjorie interviewed several persons for me. Mrs. Ellen Capach loaned her husband's large collection of railroad reports and pictures to Marjorie, and I am

very grateful to Ellen for allowing me to have these pictures and papers reproduced. Many more pictures and railroad reports could be included in this book thanks to her contributions.

I could not have used these pictures without the expertise of my daughter, Ada Marie Prill, and her camera. Her success in photographing these old and faded pictures is apparent. Ada Marie also taught me to use the computer and then edited the manuscript, making many useful suggestions. This book would have been impossible without her help.

Many thanks to Ruth Westphal for her expert help as copy editor. Hannah Malloch Rosenstraus gave me several old records that she had from her father's business with the railroad, and told me her own memories of the road. Hannah also interviewed Mel Fingado for me. Many thanks to Mel Fingado for sharing his memories with us. Carlton O'Connor, of Deposit, N.Y., wrote two stories for me. Bill Vernold told Marjorie about his father's conductor's cap.

The Damn Nuisance by Harry Archer, was of great help to me. Much of the history of the early days of the railroad would have been lost forever if Harry Archer had not preserved Ira Terry's memoirs and added much more from sources no longer available. Thanks to Edward Archer for permission to use material from his father's book, and also for allowing me to use two of Harry Archer's previously unpublished drawings.

Several excellent pictures came from L&L Photos, and Mr. Len Kilian of L&L also graciously allowed me to reproduce some of his post cards. Ethel Norwood loaned several old local pictures. Thanks to Lee Farnsworth for permission to use the D&E pass issued to L. W. Tilden and to Evelyn Murtagh for the rare picture of Dr. Brittain. Bernard Wadler of Fleischmanns came to the rescue when we needed to fill in some gaps in Chapter 10's post card album.

Three serious collectors of D&N memorabilia read the manuscript and offered suggestions.. I am grateful to Edward P. Baumgardner of Oneonta, Al Weiss of Margaretville, and John Ham of Hunter, N.Y. Photographs and tickets from the impressive Baumgardner and Ham collections will be found in the book.

Lastly, I wish to thank my publishers, Wray and Loni Rominger of Purple Mountain Press, for their efforts to preserve the history of the Catskill Mountains.

Gertrude Horton
Summer, 1989

Publisher's note: Many collectors generously offered the use of their photographs, post cards, and memorabilia for this book with the result that there were often serveral copies of the same scene or item. In each case we chose the print we thought would reproduce best. Our thanks to all who contributed.

TABLE OF CONTENTS

Kaufman's (near Andes) on a payday for the D&E construction workers. This picture was taken in 1906 before the Andes Branch was completed, and shows the narrow gauge tracks used for hauling dirt from a cut near Fowler's farm house. After the railroad was completed, the creamery and ice house in the background shut down. This card was published originally as a publicity picture announcing the opening of the railroad on November 17, 1906.
Len Kilian Collection.

Chapter 1
THE DELAWARE & EASTERN
(1904-1911)

Planning of the Railroad

After the Civil War the entire United States was gripped by "railroad fever." Hundreds of thousands of young men from the farms and villages of the nation had traveled for the first time as soldiers, and wanderlust was epidemic. There was an unprecedented demand for the fast, cheap, and convenient transportation offered by railroads. Delaware County, New York, was no exception to this trend. Men from this farming area had responded overwhelmingly to President Lincoln's calls for troops, and by the end of the Civil War, virtually all able-bodied men in the area had seen service in the Union Army—and seen parts of the country far beyond the reach of their farm wagons.

Even before the Civil War, the Erie Railroad had stopped in Hancock, but provided no service to other parts of the area. In 1871 the Ulster and Delaware skirted the northern edge of the county, connecting Arkville and Grand Gorge with the main lines serving New York City and Albany. The following year the New York, Oswego and Midland Railway (later reorganized as the New York, Ontario and Western) came to East Branch, Hancock, Walton, and Delhi. But the fertile valley of the East Branch of the Delaware remained isolated, not out of choice. Local people fer-

vently wished for a railroad and made valiant attempts to get one started, but it took a tourist with financial resources and an incipient case of railroad fever to actually bring a railroad to the East Branch Valley.

Frederick Searing, president of Searing and Company, a New York City industrial bank, and a dealer in railroad securities, enjoyed coming to the area of the East Branch of the Delaware River for summer holidays. His favorite boarding house was located in Andes, N.Y.

In the spring of 1904 he brought a group of friends to East Branch by way of the New York, Ontario & Western Railroad, which was a pleasant trip. However, the trip from there to Andes was a long and tiring one as the only transportation was by horse and carriage. It took four to five hours under the most favorable weather conditions just to get as far as Downsville, where the men spent the night. Downsville had a newspaper, hotels, stores, churches and schools, but was isolated by poor transportation. In order to secure supplies or get their produce to market the people of Downsville had two ways of reaching the O&W: either they could travel through mud or snow to East Branch (14 miles) or they could climb over Bear Spring Mountain to Walton—a route that was rocky, muddy and dangerous. The necessary winding, thousand-foot climb made that about 14 miles as well.

**Italian laborers' shanties on the Fowler farm, Andes branch. The dinkey rail
cars are hauling fill from the big cut on the Les Fowler farm in the fall of 1906.**
Photo by Margurite Fowler, E. P. Baumgardner Collection.

**Shanties on the Fowler farm. The old Delhi & Middletown roadbed of 1871 can be seen
running along the hillside in the background.**
Photo by Margurite Fowler, E. P. Baumgardner Collection.

Searing often brought rich and important friends with him, and they all dreaded that slow and bumpy trip from East Branch to Andes. This time, jokingly, one of his friends remarked, "You really ought to build a railroad from East Branch to Andes." The more Searing thought about this remark, the better the idea sounded.

On their way from Downsville to Andes, Searing and his friends realized that someone else had had the same idea. They noticed some old railroad diggings and gradings. On questioning the local people, they learned that in 1871 a railroad, called the Delhi & Middletown, had been started but did not survive the panic of 1873.

The Andes township nearly went bankrupt paying off $98,000 at 7% interest in bonds to pay for the grading for the Delhi & Middletown Railroad. After that railroad had failed, Andes fought the bonded indebtedness. The township wanted either to have the railroad constructed or relief from the debt. Between the cost of the legal fight and the high interest rate, Andes ended up paying over $370,000. They made the final payment in 1931, after paying during 60 years for a railroad that was never finished.

Later during their stay Searing and his friends heard of still another railroad failure, the Delaware Valley Railroad, officially known as the Andes and Delhi, which was started in 1898. That road also failed to get as far as Andes, although a lot of work was done. Almost 10 miles of roadbed was finished between October 8 and October 29, 1898, which was an amazing amount of work to be completed in just 21 days. There was a story told about a rough railroad camp on this road. One night there was a fatal fight over a card game between two fellow laborers. The next morning the body was tossed into a fill—no digging required and no report. Unfortunately the contractor ran out of money, the unpaid workers rebelled, and the Delaware Valley was foreclosed on July 15, 1899. Later Andes pointed to this partially finished work as a reason to build the Delaware & Eastern's Andes branch.

Searing was determined to open up this charming and prosperous country. A railroad would enable the people of the area to communicate with each other and with the rest of the world. Mail could move in and out more efficiently. The many products of the rich farmland of Delaware County could be sold in the profitable city markets, and manufactured goods from all over the world could be brought in. The isolation of

more than a century was drawing to a close, changing forever the way of life of rural families.

Later that same year Searing returned, bringing Joseph Jermyn, who owned large coal mining properties in Pennsylvania, and Russell B. Williams, an experienced railroad builder and superintendent of the Scranton Division of the New York, Ontario & Western Railroad. After exploring the region all the way from East Branch (where a railroad could connect with the already built New York, Ontario & Western) to Arkville (where it could connect with the Ulster & Delaware), they could see great business opportunities for a railroad. The new railroad would be called the Delaware & Eastern, or D&E.

The need for passenger service was obvious; travel by foot or horse and buggy was slow and uncomfortable, making it very difficult for busy farm families to go into the towns for shopping or to visit each other. However, there was a district school within walking distance (sometimes several miles) of every child. These were mostly one room schools and very few pupils ever went to any other school. A railroad would make a high school education possible for widely scattered rural residents. The enthusiasm expressed by the populace for the project made it clear that the people would use the railroad once it was built.

R. B. Williams quit the Ontario & Western Railroad to become the General Manager for the new D&E. He had long envisioned a more direct route with easier grades from the coal mines of Pennsylvania to East Branch and on to Arkville, where the railroad could connect with the Ulster & Delaware Railway. He had discussed it with Jermyn, who enthusiastically supported the plan. The Ontario & Western had some very steep grades that required a double header (a train pulled by two locomotives) and sometimes an additional pusher to get those long, long lines of gondola cars of coal up the grades. (A gondola is a railroad car with no top, a flat bottom and fixed sides that is used chiefly for hauling bulk commodities). By planning lighter grades and reduced mileage, Searing, Williams and Jermyn hoped to have a very profitable venture. The three men decided to publicly plan only the short 37.5 mile connection between East Branch and Arkville (which would all be in Delaware County), while privately planning the longer coal route.

They knew that the New York, Ontario & Western, the Ulster & Delaware and the Delaware & Hudson would not object to a connection between the O&W and the U&D, and might even welcome it. Searing even announced that he expected coal would be handled from East Branch to Arkville, enabling both roads to run more efficiently. Thus there were no objections at the beginning.

First, Searing and his associates planned to complete the East Branch to Arkville section and the Andes branch. They started at both ends, working in both directions toward Downsville, where the two work gangs were to meet. That part of the project would be about 38 miles on the main line and about nine miles more to Andes. When completed, the railroad, including sidings, would have just over 50 miles of track.

No local people or towns were asked to help pay for this railroad, as they had been for the other railroads in the area. All the D&E asked for was a right-of-way across the land and they were willing to grant certain concessions to the land owner for this right. Some of the land owners were so eager to have a railroad that they gladly gave the road the right-of-way across their land. Others were so skeptical that at first they refused to give written permission at all. They said that after the railroad had been built and operated for 30 days, then they would agree to the right-of-way. Of course, the D&E had to get permission from each and every land owner before they could proceed with any actual work. After many meetings and dickering with these people, the D&E finally had every legal land problem solved and was ready to begin the actual building of their railroad.

Methods of Construction

The building of this railroad, as with other railroads of the same era, was accomplished without the use of many labor saving devices. After the survey was completed, a very large group of men was set to work using almost nothing except hand shovels, to dig, fill, and grade the right of way. Most of the workers lived in work camps. They slept in boxcars which had been fixed up as living quarters. There were bunks in the ends of the car and a large stove for cooking and heating in the center. These cars were moved from place to place to be near the work area. The railroad also built shanties for the workers, just big enough for four or five men to sleep in. These were shabbily constructed wooden shacks, furnished with only the bare necessities. One of these shacks was built on the Malloch farm near Harvard.

Some workers hired from the local area chose to board with the farm families along the way. Most farm houses were large, and the farmers could always use the extra little bit of money to be gained by renting out an unused room or two, with as many men as would fit sleeping in each room. The men got a clean place to sleep and good fresh food, well cooked and abundant. At one time 10 to 15 workers boarded at the Fingado farm near Harvard.

Most of the laborers were immigrants from Italy who could hardly speak English. They had landed in New York City and been hired by a padrone to work on the railroad, and really did not know what to expect in this new country.

The immigrants were not even known to the railroad by their own names. Some of these laborers could speak no English and their employers could speak no Italian, so each man was assigned a number. This number was pressed into a copper disk and each man showed his disk to collect his pay. He was known by this number and was carried on the payroll by this number instead of his name. If he moved from job to job, he kept the same number.

Souvenir card shows men working with only shovels to grade back a steep bank above Union Grove. The card says, "Meet me in Downsville SATURDAY, NOV. 17, 1906 to celebrate the first through train on the D. & E. Excursion trains meet all U. & D. and O. & W. trains. Excursion rates on all roads. It will be a red letter day for the East Branch Valley never to be forgotten. See small bills for particulars."
Len Kilian Collection.

Horse drawn dump scoops were used on the level sections of ground. It took two men to operate these — one man to drive the horses and the other to operate the scoop, which had handles like a plow. The operator would press down on the handles, scrape up a load of dirt, relax the pressure on the handles and let the sharp edge of the scoop just slide over the top of the ground until they got to the dump site. There the operator would press down on the handle causing the scoop to again catch in the ground and dump the load. Going back to the diggings, the scoop was just dragged upside down.

In some places the men could use their hand shovels to load the dirt on special horse drawn wagons. The bottom of each wagon was made from heavy planks, running the length of the wagon, with a handle on each end. At the dump site, a man at each end of a plank would move it just far enough to let the dirt fall through a crack to the ground.

Sometimes extra horses were leased from the local farmers for the construction work. Oxen were also used, but oxen were more tempermental than horses. Often they would not work well with strangers, so the railroad hired the owner to drive the oxen. Archie Williams of Centerville and his oxen worked all through the construction period.

A magneto was used to set off the dynamite needed to break up the large boulders in a rock cut (a passage cut as a roadway). That made it a little safer for the men than setting off the dynamite by a fuse, as the farmers did.

It was very important that a railroad keep as much on the level as possible, so both cuts and fills were often needed. Grades made the locomotives work harder and could be dangerous to both men and machinery. When making a deep cut on a steep hill, hand shovels were the only tool used to initially cut into the bank. After the bank had been started, wooden rails were laid down to run a small car on. This car was moved either by the men or by a horse. The car was loaded and moved to the dump site, and when emptied, brought back for another load.

After a temporary iron track could be laid, a steam shovel was brought in to dig back the banks and make a wider cut. That made the work much easier. The steam shovel would load the dirt and stones on a flat car and a locomotive could take it to the place of disposal. As you can see, "life in the good old days" included a lot of hard manual labor.

Water towers were a familiar sight in the days of steam. This one is at Arkville, 1909.
William Capach Collection.

Grading a rock cut on the D&E below Shavertown. It was all pick and shovel work.
Len Kilian Collection.

The Rock Eddy bridge, here almost finished, was completed on August 14, 1906.
Ada Marie Prill Collection.

Union Grove bridge under construction. Concrete caps were put on stone piers previously built by the ill-fated Delhi and Middletown Railroad.
Stanley Horton Collection.

Early Days of the D&E

On September 14, 1905, R. B. Williams drove in the first spike near Arkville, and he was also the one who drove in the last spike at Downsville on November 17, 1906.

The first wreck on the D&E occurred on November 24, 1905, just above Margaretville, only two months and 10 days after the first spike had been driven. The first timetable was issued June 5, 1906, when construction was completed as far as Shavertown, in order to regulate the traffic between Shavertown and Arkville (14 miles).

In late 1905, as soon as a section between two towns was completed, people were demanding to ride as far as they could on their new railroad. The railroad company set planks across oil drums atop the flat cars in place of seats, and the local people rode these cars. They had to brush sparks from the engine out of their hair and they squirmed from the cinders that went down their backs, but they were happy. Soon after this,

stations and creameries were built, and by the next year the road had purchased some real coaches for their passengers to ride in.

The cost of building the D&E, up to December 31, 1907, was $1,993,838 plus $108,973 for the cost of the equipment.

Every station sign, at the outer edges of the sign, gave the distance to ARK. (Arkville) and to E.B. (East Branch). Every mile was marked by a mile post.

It was a big day for Downsville and the whole East Branch Valley when the main line was completed. Excursion trains came from both ends of the railroad to meet at Downsville for the ceremonial driving of the last spike on November 17, 1906. There were parades, band concerts, speeches of welcome, shouting and cheering. The horses reared, snorted, and slipped on the hard-packed snow. Many important men, including Frederick Searing, Henry Williams, Edward Conlon, and Judge Linn Bruce, gave impressive-sounding speeches.

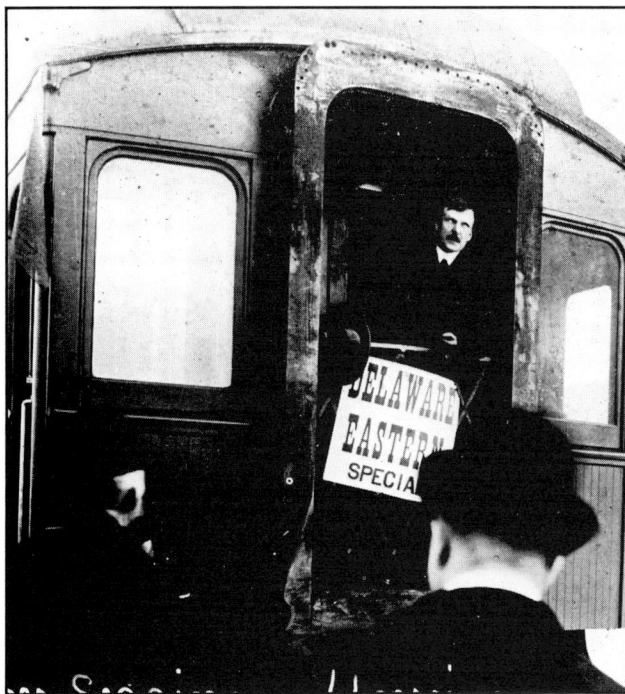

The sign reads, "FIRST TRAIN ON THE D.&E. OCT. 28 1905" This train was loaded with rail and construction materials, which had come via the U&D and was to be used south of Arkville. William Stevens, general track supervisor, is on the pilot and in the cab is John Francisco. In front with arms folded is Enos Strong. Behind him in the derby hat is Otto Wagenhorst, chief engineer, and R. B. Williams, superintendent and general manager. Clarke Sanford, editor and publisher of the Catskill Mountain News is in the light-colored overcoat. Many of the locomotive engineers and firemen started out as hostlers on the railroad.
Edward P. Baumgardner Collection.

Frederick Searing speaking at Downsville from the back of a coach on November 17, 1906, the opening of the new D&E.
Edward P. Baumgardner Collection.

The first passenger train on the D&E on Christmas Day, 1905. This was before the line was completed.
Len Kilian Collection.

General Manager Williams driving the first spike near Arkville on September 14, 1905. Standing next to him is Peter Shaver of Shavertown.
William Capach Collection.

The first section gang on the D&E, Downsville, November 29, 1906
Marjorie Fitch Collection.

Regular train service to Andes began on March 23, 1907. Andes had had telephone and telegraph service before the railroad, but mail and freight had come in by stagecoach or wagon.

As soon as regular schedules began on both the main line and the Andes branch, the D&E was given the contract to carry the U.S. Mail. From the time the mail contract began on May 13, 1907 until the last day the railroad operated, carrying the mail provided one of the few consistent sources of revenue on the D&E/D&N.

Elevation at Andes was 660 feet higher than at East Branch, but more important, Andes was 400 feet higher than Andes Junction, nine miles away. So you can see that those small locomotives had quite a climb. The original 4-4-0 locomotives (the numbers indicate the placement of the wheels on the engine) had the ability to pull only one passenger car, one baggage car and two freight cars into Andes. Engine #3, which had the 2-6-0 configuration, could haul six loaded cars up the grade.

On March 23, 1907, a cold soggy day, the first regular train service was begun on the Andes branch. Perhaps it was a sign of things to come: on March 25, 1907 an excursion train was run to celebrate the opening of the Andes branch. Coming back the last car of the train jumped the track. For the first of many times, the condition of the rails was blamed for an accident. Even at the very beginning of the road, hard luck plagued it.

In 1906 Searing announced his plans for a new railroad from Wilkes Barre, Pa., to Schenectady, N.Y., a distance of 232 miles. This would give him fast and efficient coal deliveries to New England and Eastern Canada by way of the Rutland and the Boston & Maine Railroads. He asked the New York State Railroad Commission for permits to build a northern line to be called the Schenectady & Margaretville and a southern road to be called the Hancock & Wilkes Barre Extension Railroad. The reason stated for this request was that the existing freight rates were exorbitant and that competition would help the public.

This news brought immediate protests from S.D. Coykendall for the Ulster & Delaware, L.F. Loree for the Delaware & Hudson, and T.P. Fowler for the New York, Ontario & Western roads. Both the O&W and the D&H considered that the coal trade belonged exclusively to them. They certainly did not intend to share it unless forced to do so.

The Eagle Hotel at Downsville had its own stage coach to pick up guests at the station. This long-standing landmark burned in 1987.
Marjorie Fitch Collection.

Engine #5 at Downsville Station—the detail below has been enlarged to show the old stage from the Eagle Hotel waiting for customers.
Marjorie Fitch Collection.

On December 11, 1906, the New York Railroad Commission granted both permits. Searing was now ready to proceed with his original secret plans.

The three older railroads filed a joint suit against the Railroad Commission to cancel the permits. This legal maneuver lasted through 1908 and was lost when the New York State Supreme Court ruled in favor of the Searing group.

Reorganization By Searing, May 17, 1907.

Frederick Searing was a businessman who had many interests, but his main business was banking. Searing and Company, located at 7 Wall St., New York City, had several branch banks in New York City, and they had survived the Panic of 1907. Having decided to finance the building of the extension railroads, Searing incorporated the newly completed East Branch part, called the Delaware & Eastern Railroad, with a second corporation, named the Delaware & Eastern Company. The second company was to lease the railroad and control the planned northern and southern extensions.

On May 17, 1907, Searing and Company merged the two companies and called it the Delaware & Eastern Railway Company, with a capital of $5 million and $6.5 million in first mortgage bonds. Part of the bond issue was to be used to pay off the existing bonds, and additional bonds totaling over $40 million would be issued. The cost of building the road up to December 31, 1907 had been $1,993,838 plus $108,973 for cost of equipment. At about this time the railroad employed 325 men with a payroll of $45,000 a month. Twenty men worked in the repair shop at Margaretville alone. A June 30, 1909 report showed an annual operating deficit of $236,586, but the officials believed that their financial situation was sound.

The northern section, first called the Schenectady & Southwestern Company, was soon changed to the Schenectady & Margaretville Railroad Company. The plan was for a 90-mile road from Margaretville to Schenectady, using, according to contracts which have recently come to light, the U&D tracks between Arkville and Grand Gorge.

The southern extension (the part to be in New York State) was incorporated as the Hancock & East Branch Railroad Company on July 12, 1906. Approval for the 95-mile part in Pennsylvania had not been obtained, but it was to be called the Hancock & Wilkes-Barre Extension Railroad Company. The route between East Branch and Hancock was surveyed parallel to the Ontario & Western. From Hancock they were to go to Equinunk, Honesdale, Moscow and finally on to Wilkes-Barre. The route finally decided on for the northern section was from Grand Gorge, Gilboa, Prattsville, Blenheim and on to Middleburgh. At Middleburgh they were to connect with the Middleburgh & Schoharie Railroad. Searing signed the lease for the Middleburgh & Schoharie Railroad on January 21, 1909.

By March of 1907 the surveyors were at work on the northern section. They completed the survey from Grand Gorge to Prattsville and started working between Prattsville and Gilboa. A year or more was needed to get the right-of-way purchased and hire contractors. The contract to survey and grade a section between Grand Gorge and Middleburgh was let to W. J. Oliver and Company. In the fall of 1909, Oliver started the grading, and land for the stations at Gilboa and North Blenheim was purchased. He also secured the right-of-way through these villages.

Oliver also got the contract to build two steel trestles and two tunnels. The trestle at Grand Gorge was to outshine the Lyonbrook, Cadosia and Liberty trestles of the New York, Ontario & Western Railroad. Near Prattsville, in order to avoid a very sharp 210 degree curve to the north, a tunnel was to curve through Pine Mountain and come out above Devasego Falls on Schoharie Creek.

Construction plans called for a cut 50 feet deep through Clay Hill and a concrete overpass 20 feet wide by 16 feet high on the Johnson Hollow road. There was to be a 112-foot-wide culvert and fill across the Johnson Hollow stream. A depot was planned for Prattsville on Washington Street and a 900-foot tunnel was planned about a mile below Blenheim.

Work progressed north of Grand Gorge all through the winter of 1909-1910. On October 2, 1909, F. A. Collins, chief engineer of the Dominion Construction Company, arrived at Grand Gorge. A new switch and siding were installed at Grand Gorge and more men, mules and machinery began to arrive via the U&D. About 75 men were at work on the lands of J. W. London and J. M. Cronk. By November 3, 200 men were at work between Grand Gorge and Prattsville, and soon 200 more men were at work near Gilboa.

A train of 25 carloads of dinkey engines (small locomotives especially used for hauling freight), dump cars, steam pumps and drills came in at Grand Gorge,

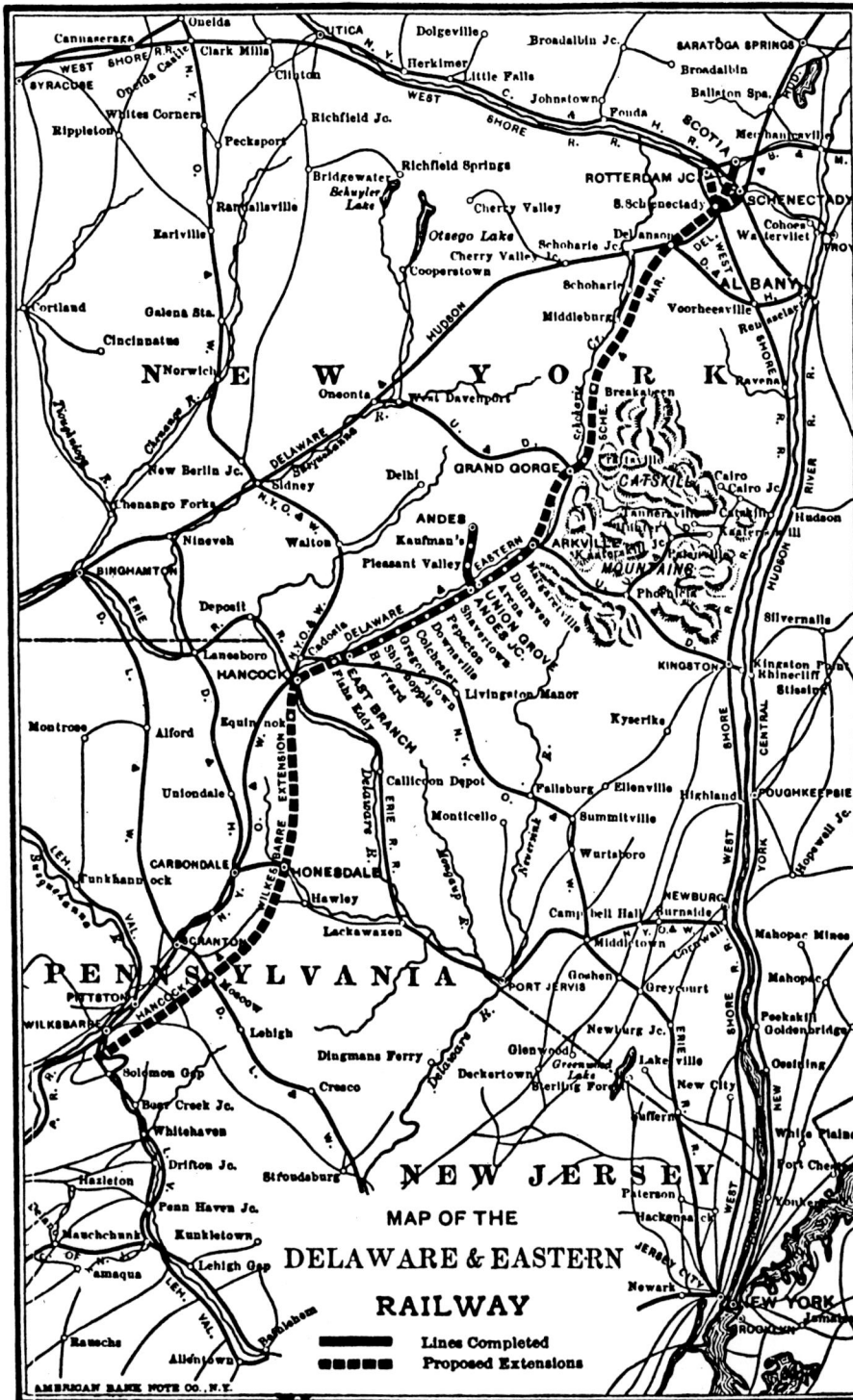

Map from POORS MANUAL OF RAILROADS—1908 showing the Delaware & Eastern in solid lines and the proposed Wilkes-Barre to East Branch and Margaretville to Schenectady extensions in dotted lines. Although some old maps show the Arkville to Grand Gorge section parallel to the Ulster & Delaware tracks, documentary evidence points to a contractual arrangement for the use of the U&D tracks, according to Edward P. Baumgardner and John Ham.

D&E Engine #3, the A. C. Fairchild, with a derailed tender at Andes.
Walter Pattberg is near the headlight.
William Capach Collection.

followed by a steady flow of cars filled with food, explosives and all other kinds of supplies.

Two steam shovels soon arrived, followed by still another larger, 50-ton one to work near Gilboa. They struggled for two weeks to get that one through the muddy countryside. It took 12 horses to pull the detached boom. The main part of this huge shovel blocked the road the entire time of the trip, and on the way it knocked down part of C. L. Tuttle's barn. In December a fourth shovel, which was to work on the Cole farm near Gilboa, had even more trouble getting there. Steam-traction engines were used to move this one, and it took them three weeks to move it. One of the traction engines skidded and was left hanging halfway over a steep cliff. If these steam shovels had been equipped with the newly-invented caterpillar tread, they could have negotiated the terrain under their own power.

Meanwhile, the blasting for the grading was not going smoothly. One blast loosened a 40-foot bank above a steam shovel, and another steam shovel had to be moved in to dig the first one out. Another blast sent a rock flying through the air. It crashed through the roof of Charles Hare's house and landed on a rocking chair, where Mrs. Hare had been sitting only a few moments before. Still another blast sent 50 tons of earth rolling down a hill. A milk house that happened to be in the way was spread all over the field beyond. One large boulder that was set free by a steam shovel rolled down a hill and killed a workman. It seemed that fate was against this extension on the D&E.

Then the weather showed what it could do. On December 25, 1909, 20 inches of snow fell, followed by many days of extreme cold, high winds and more snow. That was followed by a January thaw that carried away bridges and equipment and bogged down all the machinery.

On February 9, 1910, all construction came to a standstill because no money was coming from the D&E. This seemed to confirm rumors that Searing and Company was in deep trouble. The contractor refused to do any more work until he had been paid

Construction locomotives at Prattsville for work on the D&E extension in 1909.
Edward P. Baumgardner Collection.

$250,000 for work already completed. In addition he refused to order the bridge materials or start the boring of the tunnels, and he also sued the D&E for the amount of his claim.

There were chaotic conditions all along the abandoned right-of-way as the penniless workers drifted away, leaving unpaid board bills. Stables of mules were left to be cared for by the neighboring farmers. Machinery was abandoned, buried by drifts of snow, and anything that could be carried away simply disappeared. Many farmers had their fields ruined by all the digging and blasting, but it was of no use to try to collect damages.

The financial trouble all started when Searing entrusted bonds worth $4.5 million to a bond salesman who was supposed to sell $3.5 million in England for a commission of $85,000 in bonds. He dumped the whole amount on the American market. Searing protested and tried to stop this move. The Supreme Court issued a writ of attachment, and the newspapers picked up the story. The depositors of Searing's bank were still a little nervous from the Panic of 1907, and a run began on the bank. Searing couldn't cover the demands and had to close the bank. In March of 1910 the brokerage firm of Searing and Company closed its doors and declared bankruptcy. The railroad was the only tangible thing to survive, and it was forced into receivership on March 10, 1910. Andrew Moreland and Walter Trowbridge were appointed receivers. It was reported that on June 2, 1910, bonds of the D&E worth $30,000 were sold for $200.

On August 16, 1911, under foreclosure proceedings, the railway was sold for $150,000 to William Seif, who represented the bond holders. The road was reorganized and incorporated as the Delaware & Northern Railroad Company on October 14, 1911.

Thus ended the grand dream of Searing's railroad empire, of a railroad from the coal fields of Pennsylvania to the factories and cities of the north.

The collapse of the Delaware & Eastern extensions must have been a relief to the other three railroads, and it ended for all time efforts to build any more new railroads from the Pennsylvania coal regions. If the D&E had succeeded, it certainly would have siphoned off a lot of profitable business from all three roads. The Ulster & Delaware, the Delaware & Hudson and the New York, Ontario & Western Railroads could now concentrate on their own operations.

If the Schenectady & Margaretville had been finished, it would have cost New York City a lot of money when reservoirs were built in that area. New York City would have had to relocate the railroad to higher ground, as they had to do for the Ulster & Delaware at Ashokan.

As long as Searing had control of the railroad, the company had a plush office on Wall Street. The office was then moved to 10 Bridge St., and finally, on February 6, 1913, the headquarters were changed to the old creamery building at Margaretville. That was quite a comedown for the office workers.

The concrete underpass at Johnson Hollow, Prattsville, built in 1910 for Searing's planned Schenectady & Margaretville Railroad Co. This photograph, taken during construction, shows a light rail above to allow donkey carts to haul fill. This underpass was demolished by the Delaware County Highway Department in 1988 because of low headroom.
Arthur Rikard Collection.

Note that a portion of the roadbed has slipped away on the newly built D&E between
East Branch and Harvard. Such washouts were common.
William Capach Collection.

D&E Engine #1, the F. F. Searing, at Archer's feed store at Andes in 1907. In front are Les Avery, John
Fowler, Tom Chamberlain, Louis Sanford, Clare Cowan, two women, and Roma Fitch with a shovel.
Marjorie Fitch Collection.

D&E Engine #4, the H. M. George, at East Branch in 1906. Note the large (62") drivers.
Stanley Horton Collection.

The H. M. George arrived at East Branch via the O&W for delivery to the D&E.
William Capach Collection.

Way freight Engine #3 at Arena siding, waiting for a passenger train (Engine #5) on April 6, 1909.

A way freight train carried less-than-carload shipments, or it might carry mixed carload and less-than-carload shipments.
William Capach Collection.

A Delaware & Eastern train at the Margaretville station.
E. P. Baumgardner Collection.

D&E Engine #2 with Andes branch way freight at the Union Grove Station on April 6, 1909.
William Capach Collection.

D&E station at Shavertown showing the main track and siding.
Merlin Twaddell Collection.

Construction of D&E railroad and creamery at Shavertown.
John Ham Collection.

**D&E engine coming to East Branch. Steep banks caused trouble
with mud slides in spring and with snow in winter.**
Marjorie Fitch Collection.

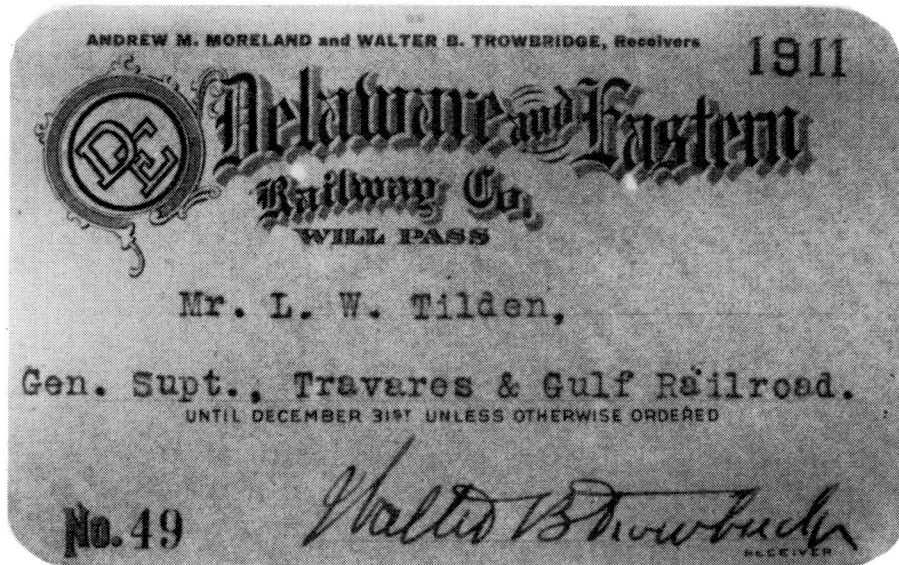

ANDREW M. MORELAND and WALTER B. TROWBRIDGE, Receivers

1911

Delaware and Eastern Railway Co.

WILL PASS

Mr. L. W. Tilden,

Gen. Supt., Travares & Gulf Railroad.

UNTIL DECEMBER 31ST UNLESS OTHERWISE ORDERED

No. 49

All railroads issued complimentary passes to officals of other railroads when asked. This pass was issued to General Superintendent L. W. Tilden of the Travares & Gulf Railroad in Florida.

Lee Farnsworth Collection. All publication rights reserved. Used by permission.

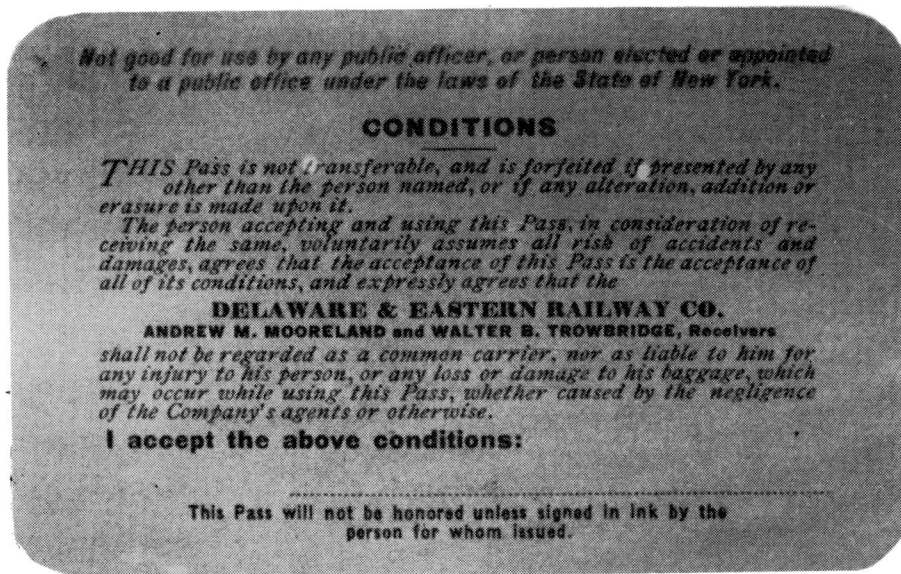

Not good for use by any public officer, or person elected or appointed to a public office under the laws of the State of New York.

CONDITIONS

THIS Pass is not transferable, and is forfeited if presented by any other than the person named, or if any alteration, addition or erasure is made upon it.

The person accepting and using this Pass, in consideration of receiving the same, voluntarily assumes all risk of accidents and damages, agrees that the acceptance of this Pass is the acceptance of all of its conditions, and expressly agrees that the

DELAWARE & EASTERN RAILWAY CO.
ANDREW M. MOORELAND and WALTER B. TROWBRIDGE, Receivers

shall not be regarded as a common carrier, nor as liable to him for any injury to his person, or any loss or damage to his baggage, which may occur while using this Pass, whether caused by the negligence of the Company's agents or otherwise.

I accept the above conditions:

_____

This Pass will not be honored unless signed in ink by the person for whom issued.

D&N Engine #1 was an ex-South Indiana, built in 1902 and reconditioned by Baldwin Locomotive Works in 1911. This is a picture taken by Baldwin.

Stanley Horton Collection.

Chapter 2
THE DELAWARE & NORTHERN

The First Receivership
(1911-1921)

Reorganization and Repair

The receivers' board of directors hired an expert appraiser named Jabez T. O'Dell to look over the D&N. He stated that the road had to have some extensive repairs made. It was costing $400 more per mile to operate than it took in.

The new directors came from Pittsburgh banks that held bonds in the old company. They decided to advance money to put the railroad in first-class condition, and accepted preferred stock in place of bonds.

Bank gravel had been used as track ballast throughout the Delaware & Eastern when it was built and by now it needed quite a lot of work to make it safe. The roadbed was reballasted where it was needed.

Additional locomotives and shop equipment were purchased and all surplus equipment was sold to other roads. A lot of freight cars, which had been bought new in 1906 and never used, were sold at this time.

Men from left to right are Clare Cowan, Roma Fitch, Gus Williams, E. Pennett, and Les Avery. Flags on the engine are to celebrate Independence Day, 1912.

Marjorie Fitch Collection.

D&N Engine # 4 at East Branch in 1915.
Stanley Horton Collection

Filling in Muir's trestle, 1915.
Edward P. Baumgardner Collection.

Trestles Filled During the First Receivership

When building the Andes branch, the D&E first built a long wooden trestle about two miles below Andes called Muir's trestle because it crossed the Muir farm. The trestle was 450 feet long, 45 feet high, and 190,000 feet of hemlock timber was used in its construction. There were water barrels placed the length of the trestle for fire protection. The trestle was completed in March, 1907, but by 1914 the state inspectors were already questioning the safety of the weathered wooden timbers.

Business was good at that time, so company officials decided to fill the whole area beneath the trestle with dirt. Work started on the fill in June, 1915. This was a big job, considering that except for a steam shovel and a locomotive, all work was done by hand. The dump cars used on this job were operated by air pressure supplied by the locomotive. These cars dumped their load from the side of the cars directly to the fill below.

The dirt from the banks along the track was cleared back, and all the cuts were widened. During the life of the Andes branch this widening of the cuts and removal of the steep banks saved the road a lot of maintenance in the spring and winter. Mud and rock slides in the spring (and after every hard rain) and snow drifts in the winter plagued the main line for the life of the road.

The filling of this long trestle was the talk of everyone in the area. Newspapers reported that company officals were planning an extension of the road to Delhi and Bovina. Everyone seemed to have high hopes for their railroad. It is too bad that this prosperity could not have lasted.

After their success in filling the big Muir's trestle, the railroad managers decided to make a fill in place of the old wooden trestle that extended from the north side of Beaverkill railroad bridge at East Branch to the higher ground along the Delaware River. This would please the state inspector and save on maintenance as well. The trestle was long but not very high, so it was decided to get all the dirt for the fill from the steep upper bank near the railway's old water tank. A steam shovel was moved in, and Engine #5 was assigned to the task. It was a much easier job than the one they had at Muir's trestle.

Engine #6 at Muir's trestle — Walter Pattberg, Sam Fullerton, Ernie Barnhart, Roma Fitch.
Stanley Horton Collection.

D&N steam shovel widening the cuts on the Andes branch to get fill for Muir's trestle in 1915. Walter Pattberg is the shovel operator.
Both Marjorie Fitch Collection.

The culvert being built under Muir's trestle.

Filling Muir's trestle. Dump cars were operated by compressed air supplied by the engine.

The East Branch trestle before filling operations. It ran north from the railroad bridge.

A view of the concrete mixer and forms for the culvert under the fill at Muir's.

D&N steam shovel at work getting fill for the East Branch trestle.

Engine #5 with the D&N work train filling the trestle at East Branch

From the collections of Stanley Horton, Marjorie Fitch and William Capach.

The End of the First Receivership

In the summer of 1916 the Interstate Commerce Commission under the order of the U.S. Government undertook the job of evaluating all railroads in the United States. The D&N was inventoried, measured and appraised. Even every rail was recorded, including the date of rolling. After much bureaucratic red tape and cost to the taxpayer, it was decided that the D&N was worth $1,505,770, including the Andes branch at $190,273. You can see that the count was exact, right down to the last three dollars.

In the summer of 1917 the United States Government was trying to sell war bonds to raise money to carry on World War I. They fitted up flat cars with samples of the heavy equipment they were using, to show the people why so much more money was needed. These flat cars traveled from railroad to railroad. One traveled the length of the D&N, and people supported their country by buying as many bonds as they could afford.

There wasn't the chance for the D&N to build up revenues that there was on most railroads. There were no steel mills, pottery plants or other big businesses. Big-time coal hauling was now only a broken dream. Lumber had been rafted down the Delaware for 50 or 60 years before the railroad came to town, and now the acid factories had stripped the mountains of all the trees left by previous loggers. Wooden mine props had been cut and shipped to Scranton, Pa., for the coal mines near there. Soon all the logs of the right size and strength were stripped from nearby forests. A lot of hemlock trees had been cut for their bark, since bark was used for tanning leather. The large-scale lumber business was gone forever.

There was a barrel-stave factory at Arena that at one time shipped four carloads a week. There was an excelsior plant at Shavertown and a mill in Downsville that made shingles. These had been small operations, and most were now gone. The combined effects of all the cutting left no chance for a factory that used wood to be able to locate on this railroad.

However, the dairy feed tonnage produced a lot of business. Before the railroad farmers usually "dried up" their cows in winter and fed them mostly hay. Now they were milking year around, and soon they discovered the boost in milk production that feeding grain would give. Feed stores opened in every town. Also, the dairy farmers were now using commercial fertilizer and lime. So the dairy farmers helped the rail revenue a lot.

One other change in the rural way of life helped boost rail freight. The villagers had often burned green or partly-seasoned wood in the winter, and there was constant worry about a chimney full of soot and creosote catching fire. As soon as the railroad made hard coal available in steady and cheap quantities, these people converted to coal-burning furnaces and burned coal in their kitchen stoves. With coal, they could keep a fire going for hours and stay warm all night without much danger of accidents. The tons of coal burned by all the people and businesses in the area accounted for a lot of gondola cars full of coal being moved on the D&N.

Most of the coal hauled on the D&N to supply the general public was anthracite, but the creameries and acid factories burned soft coal. After the Andes branch closed down, it took two trucks full time just to bring soft coal from Delhi to the Co-op Creamery at Andes, so you can guess the amount of coal hauled by the D&N to supply the creameries and acid factories all along the length of the railroad. Of course, many farmers still burned the wood they cut from their own wood lots.

The little road managed to meet expenses from 1911 to 1918. The biggest money-maker was the dairy business. The D&N owned seven milk cars that they kept busy, and sometimes they had to borrow cars from the connecting roads. This was originating freight, so the D&N got the lion's share of the revenue.

Any surplus money was paid to the preferred stockholders. The last dividend of $15,000 was paid in 1918.

The loss of small businesses all along the road and the general downturn of the national economy after World War I made the deficits mount up quickly after 1918. The situation deteriorated very rapidly until in 1920 a suit was brought by a large coal company, joined by some of the railroad's smaller creditors. The D&N was forced by this suit into a new receivership. On March 16, 1921 president Moreland and superintendent J. J. Welch were appointed receivers.

The Second Receivership
(1921-1928)

Financial Crisis

As soon as Moreland and Welch took over as receivers in 1921, they realized that some drastic measures had to be taken to keep the road going. The poor railroad was in bad financial shape.

When the people of the Delaware Valley realized that their railroad was in trouble, they tried to come to the rescue. Most of the tax assessors, except in the town of Hancock, reduced the road's taxes. The employees agreed to a cut in wages which would save the road $12,000 per year.

Then a federal judge ruled that the employees must take a 20% cut in wages and the road must sell $20,000 in receivers' certificates. If this was not done he would shut down the road.

People along the railroad bought the $20,000 worth of certificates. The workers were already working for low wages, and when they heard that they were supposed to take another 20% cut, the train crews refused. They couldn't see how they could take care of their families with any less money. A compromise was finally reached when they all met at Margaretville, and the road was saved one more time.

The D&N Officals Meet with Governor Al Smith

In the early 1920s Governor Al Smith became concerned about the number of fatal accidents occurring at railroad-highway crossings. Ever since the family car had become popular, the accident rate had increased every year. Smith hired an expert to survey the railroads of New York State and report the crossings most needing to be changed. None of the railroads were notified that this was being done. When the survey was completed, the governor sent invitations to the presidents, trustees, and receivers of all the railroads operating in New York State, to meet with him at the state capitol building. The reason for the meeting was not disclosed.

President James Welch received an invitation. He was extremely surprised and also apprehensive at receiving such an invitation. Welch and Ira Terry ar-rived at the appointed time and were ushered in, along with officials of all the other railroads, to meet the governor. They were all handed a brochure explaining the reason for the meeting. The brochure listed all the crossings thought to be the most dangerous in the state, detailed how each was to be changed, and estimated costs.

Governor Smith explained that he understood that the elimination of grade crossings would be very expensive and a hardship for some of the roads. He assured everyone that the state was willing to loan money to the railroads that might need help, then asked for comments from those present.

Many got up and announced that they would try to cooperate with the state in this matter. Mr. Loree of the Delaware & Hudson agreed to the need, but objected to the crossings selected by the experts. He said that he could point out several crossings more dangerous than those that had been chosen for elimination. President Welch was relieved that for once his road was not in serious trouble with the state. Not a single crossing on the D&N had been selected for elimination. The trip back home was much happier than the one going, to answer an unexplained summons to meet the governor.

More Financial Trouble

In 1924, the station at Shinhopple burned to the ground. Since the D&N could not afford a new station, they built a cubicle that would only hold about four persons. It was just a place to stand and get out of the weather.

By 1925 the road was in desperate financial trouble again. The profitable cauliflower transportation had been lost to trucks. Ice-refrigerator cars had been used to keep the cauliflower in good shape on the long journey to the city. Now trucks picked up the cauliflower, at an auction block in Margaretville. It was near enough to the railroad that the trainmen could smell the cauliflower, but they got not one cent of revenue. The railroad went from a seasonal high of 14 cars in one day to transport cauliflower to zero. Some agricultural produce was still being shipped by rail, but every year the road had less and less business.

D&N Station at Shinhopple which burned in 1924. Finances were so bad that the line could afford only the cubicle below to replace it.
Collections of William Capach and Stanley Horton.

In former years, much of the profit had been from the creameries; now tank trucks carried the milk. The railroad no longer needed all those ice-refrigerator cars. Most of the creameries were no longer owned by the railroad, which was nearly out of the ice business as a result. Since that was never profitable by itself, the road might have been glad to be rid of it, but losing the business it represented was disastrous.

Passenger usage of the road dropped off because so many people were buying automobiles, and more and more hard surface roads were being built for the growing numbers of automobiles and trucks. Desperate measures had to be taken.

The Andes branch had not been profitable for quite some time, so that was shut down in the later part of March, 1925. That did not help much. Gone but not forgotten was the only railroad to get to Andes. Andes had seriously gone into debt to get the Delhi & Middletown Railroad to come to their village, and that road was never built, leaving Andes with a crushing debt and no railroad. It had not cost them anything to get the D&E to come to Andes, but now once again they were without a railroad.

The right-of-way of the railroad reverted back to the orginal owners for just the cost of drawing up the transfer deeds. Big trucks took over the business of hauling feed and coal to this busy town. The new con-

crete highway built in 1922 between Andes and Margaretville, along with all the other improved roads in the area, made year-long travel by car and truck possible.

Brill Car

The cost of running a locomotive was high for the amount of business that the road now had, so the owners decided to buy a Brill-built motor car. This was a self-propelled, combined passenger, express and railway post office car, and was purchased in February of 1926. It proved to be the best investment ever made by the D&N. If, from the begining of the road, all other equipment had run as well and been as cost-effective as the Brill car, this story might have had a different ending.

The Brill Car was 65 feet long, with a six-cylinder 250-HP Winton Special automotive-type gasoline motor. It had five gears forward and five in reverse with manual shift and direct drive to the front truck. It cost $28,750 new, and the railroad claimed it saved them $30,000 per year operating expense. In use from February 25, 1926 to October 19, 1942, it was the last thing that moved on the D&N. Walter Pattberg went to Philadelphia to take delivery of the new car and was coached on the way back by a Brill representative

named Day, who was hired by the manufacturer to train the new owners in the care and handling of their brand-new machine. James Welch and Pop Philips met the car in Newark, N.J. The car was met by a group of U&D officials at Kingston, who wanted to see how the Brill Car would take the grades on their road. The car encountered no trouble whatsoever on the grades and a group of proud men reached Margaretville with a piece of NEW equipment.

Pop Philips was senior engineer, so he was first in line to bid in the position of engineer of the new Brill Car. He had never learned to drive an automobile, and he was unable to master the automotive type of controls. So Clarence Cowan, Roma Fitch and Joe Rider were the operators. Most of the time Harry Odell was the postal clerk.

It was said that the revenue from the U.S. Government for postal service paid the total expense of running the Brill Car.

The Brill Car was always a dull red color, probably never having more than a primer coat of paint. The D&N tracks were noted for their poor condition.

Brill Car showing engineer, postal, express, and passenger compartments.
Stanley Horton Collection.

The crew of the Brill Car—Raymond Winner (express), Howard Liddle (conductor), Harry Odell (mail clerk), and Clare Cowan (engineer).
William Capach Collection.

The Brill Car passes test bore sites for the proposed dam above Downsville.
John Ham Collection.

D&N Motor Car #10 (Brill Car) at Arkville turntable.
Photo by George Phelps, John Ham Collection.

Brill Car leaving East Branch on October 17, 1942 — the day of abandonment. Howard Liddle and Clare Cowan are on the ground and Harry Odell is in the open doorway.
William Capach Collection.

The Brill Car wreck with pupils aboard on September 5, 1934
Stanley Horton Collection.

John Ham Collection.

D&N combination coach showing the express and postal doors.

This joint was on the main line in front of the side entrance of the Margaretville shop in December 1941. Employees said many such gaps developed along the tracks toward the last days of the line. The wheels of the Brill Car showed the effects of slamming through such places.
William Capach Collection.

Speed was limited to 20 MPH. The lurching, swaying motion of the car soon earned it the nickname of "Red Heifer." The Brill Car's schedule was the same as the old steam passenger train. It started at Downsville in the morning, going to Arkville, and there used the turntable. This turntable was moved by human power. The trainmen would get down in the pit and literally push the car or engine around. However, it was geared well and this was not really a hard job.

Later the car made a run to East Branch, and back to Arkville, then back to Downsville to wait for the next day. This schedule enabled the pupils of Margaretville High School from Arena to Margaretville to use the "Red Heifer" as a school bus.

Although the Brill Car was more reliable and had fewer accidents than any other of the D&N's motive power, there was one accident that could have been serious. On Sept. 5, 1934, when the Brill Car, with a load of school pupils was about one mile north of Arena, it flipped over on its left side. It happened at Lilly Pond and only the slow speed of the car kept it from sliding or rolling into the pond. There was a pile of school pupils, lunch pails, and books, but most of the kids were not even bruised and were back in school the next day.

The Brill Car fared well also. Within three days, after a checkup in the shop, it was back in service. The old combination car, pulled by a locomotive, was put in service for those three days. This accident was an isolated incident. The car seldom decided to leave the tracks. It was more trustworthy than any of the other rolling stock.

Near the floor of the postal compartment there was an escape hatch, just large enough for a man to get through to the driver's compartment. There was never an accident when this had to be used.

Whenever the Brill Car decided to go off the rails, it had a disconcerting habit: the brake chain would go slack. There was nothing anyone could do but sit it out until the car bumped to a stop. Harry Odell, the regular postal clerk on the car, said he could tell when the car gave a wrong kind of lurch that it was going to leave the rails.

The Brill Car had a very loud air horn and the blasts from the horn could bounce for miles along the mountains and valleys of the Delaware River. The mountain masses and the width of the valleys seemed to have the correct acoustical properties for relaying the sounds. It was said that the early Dutch feared the rumble of thunder echoing through the mountains, and that prevented them from settling this area until later.

One time the front-drive truck gave out completely and the railroad secured one by running a want ad in *Railroad* magazine. The rails on the D&N were mostly only 65-pound rail with replacement rails of 90-pound rail. Toward the end of the D&N the rails in some places developed as much as four inch gaps. The wheels of the Brill Car were in bad shape from slamming through such places.

No one knows for sure where the faithful Brill Car disappeared to. It was on a siding all by itself, without any tracks except those it was standing on, after the abandonment of the road. It was said that Rosoff refused to sell the Brill Car with the rest of the equipment. He wanted to make it into a private rail car for his own use. After World War II, when all the local people could settle down to normal life, they realized that it was no longer there. "Must have been sold to another railroad," was the best guess.

The purchase of the Brill Car saved the railroad a lot of money over all the years that it was in service. It was just a case of too little and too late.

End of the Second Receivership

In September of 1928, three of the road's biggest creditors joined together to petition the Federal Court for permission to have the road discontinued. They were the Pittsburgh & Shawmut Coal Company, the Title Guarantee & Trust Company of Pittsburgh and J. J. Jermyn. All had a lot of money invested in this railroad. Jermyn had had an interest in the railroad from the very beginning. He was one of three men who

helped plan the railroad in 1904. It was a sad day when J. J. Jermyn no longer had any hope for this road. He had been a faithful friend throughout all these years. On October 2, 1928, after a hearing in Albany, N.Y., the ruling was that the road must be sold at public auction unless the receivers could find someone to buy the road and continue to operate it.

The flood of October, 1932 washed away the track near the Dry Brook bridge at Arkville.
Stanley Horton Collection.

Rosoff and the D&N
(1929-1942)

Sam Rosoff, a New York City subway contractor, bought the D&N, taking charge on January 1, 1929. Mr. Rosoff reorganized the railroad, changing the name from Delaware & Northern Railroad to Delaware & Northern Railway Company. It still held the same name at the closing on Oct. 17, 1942.

New York City, which was chronically short of water, had built its first great upstate reservoir at Ashokan in 1914. At that time 17 miles of the Ulster & Delaware Railroad had to be relocated. In 1923 the Gilboa Dam was built, and still the city needed more water. By 1928 almost everyone along the Delaware Valley was talking about the dam to be built on the East Branch. Test borings had been made. People were speculating on how far up a hillside the water from the new dam would come or how far up a hollow the water would go. Some were hoping the new dam would take their property, and some were swearing that they would never give up their homes for a dam.

It was rumored at the time that Rosoff had purchased the railroad in hopes of landing a fat contract from New York City when the talked-of dam at Downsville was started. President Welch had mentioned to Rosoff the potential profitability of owning a railroad at the dam site, perhaps hoping that somehow the railway could be kept operating a little longer.

As soon as Rosoff reorganized the railroad instead of dismantling it as expected, the officials of New York City were quite upset. Rosoff had moved before the politicians knew what was happening, and it was all his. The newspapers reported everything that he planned or they thought he might be planning. Of course he knew that New York City would have to build the dam sooner or later.

Owning the only railroad would allow him to underbid competitors for the big job of building tunnels under the Catskills for the water to flow through. He would be able to bring in all the heavy machinery by rail and unload only a few feet from the tunnel he hoped to dig. His nickname was "Subway Sam." New York City officials groaned as they could see the $70,000 that he had paid for the road multiplied many times over. At the very least the city would have to buy and relocate the part of the railroad in the area to be flooded by the reservoir.

Only a few months after Rosoff's takeover, the stock market crash came, and the nation was plunged into the worst Depression in its history. New York could not take on the massive job of reservoir-building until the economy improved, so both sides had to wait, not knowing that the Depression would continue for a decade and would be immediately followed by another World War.

All through the 1930s Rosoff poured a lot of his own money into the railroad to keep it going. He seemed to enjoy owning his own little D&N. Throughout the Depression, when employment was scarce, D&N employees had jobs.

New York City officials continued to feel nervous. They could see the price going up every week, but they didn't have the money to act immediately. Whatever his motives, Rosoff did make quite a lot of much-needed improvements. There were many carloads of new rails, new ties, and spikes. He reroofed and painted all the stations for the first time since they were built, and put a lot of new equipment in the Margaretville shops. He talked of building a new creamery and of extending the railroad to Wilkes-Barre, to the coal fields. Month by month, the thirsty city worried about Rosoff and the building of the dam.

The need for maintenance and repair continued. Floods in 1932 took out part of the trestle at the north end of the Dry Brook bridge at Arkville. In the spring of 1942 the flood waters again gave the D&N a lot of trouble. The mud and stones that washed down the brooks covered the tracks with four feet of rubble in some places. At Cat Hollow, the stones and mud that swept into the kitchen of the Bogart farmhouse were so heavy that the kitchen floor gave way, and the kitchen stove landed in the cellar along with the rocks. The house was so near the tracks that, when it was relieved of all that weight, it swung around and sat directly on the tracks.

Finally, the city could no longer put off its plans to build a new reservoir. The economy had improved, and it was evident that the U.S. might get involved in the war in Europe, bringing a big increase in the price of everything. New York City needed the water as soon as possible; it had to get that railroad and build the dam. So in 1942 a settlement was made, but by that time the United States was involved in World War ll, and no construction materials were available for civilian projects. The timing could hardly have been worse, but no one involved in the project believed that the war would last very long. Ironically at a time when gasoline shortages and rationing would have made rail travel economically attractive once more, the D&N ceased operations. The timing was unfortunate for the city as well — by the time construction could begin, the roadbed had been without maintenance so long that it was useless.

During the last few days of the life of the D&N, one of the new heavyweight, 100-ton hopper cars arrived fully loaded with coal for a customer on the D&N. The car was received at East Branch from the Ontario & Western Railroad, but as soon as it rolled onto the D&N's tracks, it began breaking rails. The D&N crew had to unload the coal into smaller gondolas in order to deliver it to their customer.

October 17, 1942, was a sad day for many people from one end of the old D&N to the other. Even the weather reflected the mood of the people at the loss of their beloved road. It was a cloudy, rainy day and the temperature only got to 44° at one o'clock in the afternoon. Motor car #10, the Brill Car, made its last passenger run. Some of the men had decorated it with bunting, placing an American flag on the rear of the car. Among several people who took this last ride were Kate Lattin and John Francisco. They had also made the trip on the first train to run over the Delaware & Eastern in 1906. The workers returned sadly to their homes, because to all intents and purposes their beloved D&N was now a part of history.

However there was one piece of unfinished business. A partly unloaded box car stood on the siding at the GLF store at Margaretville. So the Brill Car was brought out on Monday the 19th of October to haul the now-empty box car to Arkville and transfer it to the U&D. The D&N's usual luck still held true. Halfway to Arkville, the Brill Car ran out of gas.

Rosoff sold the 19 miles of the railroad that New York City needed for $200,000, leaving him the rest of the road to sell for scrap. About 45,000 tons of iron was sold, at a high price, and was used to build weapons for the war. At the same time, Rosoff was awarded a profitable contract to construct 15 miles of tunnel for New York City, and another contract with the U.S. Government to build the third set of locks for the Panama Canal.

The railroad stations were sold to the highest bidder and the land was returned to the original owners. Rosoff probably made no money on the sale of his railway, as he had put a lot of his own money into it every year that he owned it. Had the railroad stayed in business just a little longer, it probably would have been very busy. The war brought gasoline rationing and a complete moratorium on the building of new trucks and cars for civilian use, so once again as much freight as possible was shipped by rail.

The Pepacton Dam was begun right after World War ll and was finished by 1955. New York City tore up the part of the railroad it had purchased, which by this time would have required major repairs. By the time construction began it was more economical to use trucks to transport the material needed to build the dam.

A railroad lives and dies just like the people that it serves. Some live a long time and others die young. The D&N inspired a lot of local pride in all the towns that it served. It filled a great need of the people of the Delaware Valley who loved their railroad. It is gone but not forgotten.

A sad day for the D&N: the Brill Car makes its last stop at East Branch on October 17, 1942.
William Capach Collection.

A Delaware & Northern Album

No. 3 between Margaretville and Arkville.
Edward P. Baumgardner Collection.

Engine #2 at Margaretville.
L&L Photos Collection.

Engine #3 steamed up and on display for a rail-fan trip which stopped at Arkville on September 20, 1936.
John Ham Collection.

Engine #4 at Margaretville – Bill Vernold and Guy Sheable are on the tender.
William Capach Collection.

Engine #5 at Andes Junction on June 29, 1915.
William Capach Collection.

Engine #7 never worked right while the D&N had it.
William Capach Collection.

Engine #7 being scrapped at the Margaretville yard. October 2, 1936.
L&L Photos Collection.

Engine #10 on the wye at East Branch. The wye consisted of tracks positioned in the shape of a letter Y, enabling a locomotive to reverse direction without using a turntable.
Photo by Walter Ruegger, John Ham Collection.

Engine #10 with way freight crossing the East Branch railroad bridge just before crossing Route 17.
L&L Photos Collection.

Passenger Coach #84 at Margaretville. July 4, 1937.
L&L Photos Collection.

**D&N Combination Coach #81. May 30, 1938. In later years it was used only when
the Brill Car was in the shop.**
L&L Photos Collection.

Engine #10 had a 2-6-0 wheel arrangement and the reputation of being the best engine on the line (Margaretville, May 30, 1938). It was scrapped after the D&N shut down.

L&L Photos Collection.

Interior view of a locomotive showing gauges and firebox door. This is an O&W class V2 engine—a D&N engine would have been similar.

William Capach Collection.

The D&N shops at Margaretville, 1938.
Photo by George Phelps, John Ham Collection.

Engines #3 and #10 inside the Margaretville shop on Christmas Day, 1941. Mr. and Mrs. Robert Liddle are on the pilot of #3, and #10 is ready to go.
William Capach Collection.

**The station at East Branch. This view shows the two O&W tracks
and a D&N train waiting to pull out.**
William Capach Collection.

Chapter 3
RURAL LIFE IN THE RAILROAD ERA

East Branch, New York

The community of East Branch was a typical shopping center in the early 1900s. Perhaps a description of East Branch will help the reader understand how the railroads changed the lives of the people that it touched.

East Branch was a centrally-located, bustling community where the D&N and O&W met and shared a railroad station. No one would believe now how busy it was, and how many activities took place there. Most of the business places have burned down over the years, and very little is left to show the former importance of the village. East Branch is not unique in this, as most rural towns have lost out to larger centers and shopping malls.

Let us go back in time and look at this busy, important village. First of all, because it was at the junction of Routes 17 and 30, it was more convenient for people living in nearby small villages and farms to shop there than at Hancock, Downsville, or Roscoe. Horse and buggy or farm-wagon travel was difficult, and East Branch was near at hand. Furthermore, it had had the O&W railroad since the early 1870s to bring in supplies for this farming center.

East Branch could furnish almost anything its populace needed. S. N. Wheeler had a hardware store, built in 1906 and still standing. Later, this building was used for many years as the East Branch Fire Hall. Across the way was the White Building, where a clothing store mostly sold men's outerwear. Next door was the Jones Hotel, which burned down sometime between 1907 and 1910 and was replaced by the three-story Delaware Hotel, which is another of the few commercial buildings still standing. It is now a private home. East Branch was a very busy place in those days.

Across the railroad tracks was Hall's store and home (all one building) with a tall tower on the far end. It was said that J. W. Hall built the tower so that he could climb to the top and survey most of his holdings. The store had a set of drive-on scales out front for weighing bulk feed or coal. The farmer drove the wagon on empty, recorded the weight, loaded the wagon and reweighed it to get the weight of the load. Sometimes a farmer would get the empty wagon weighed with him on the driver's seat and try to get the loaded wagon weighed standing alongside it. That way he would get his own weight in coal or feed free. No one got away with that often. There were two other scales in town. One was in front of the feed store and the other was in back of the station.

Inside the store was almost anything people wanted to purchase. Hall's store sold all kinds of groceries and had a large coffee grinder to grind fresh roasted coffee beans. Here you could buy clothing for the whole family, including shoes and rubber boots, or you could buy material by the yard, thread, buttons, etc. to

Main Street in East Branch —
Wheeler's hardware store is on the
left, the maple trees are still young.
Marjorie Fitch Collection.

Jones' Hotel in East Branch. It
burned down sometime between 1907
and 1910
Ethel Norwood Collection.

The lounge in Jones' Hotel. Brass
spitoons were the order of the day.
Ethel Norwood Collection.

Main Street, East Branch — Delaware Hotel is on the right and the railroad tracks are in the foreground.
Marjorie Fitch Collection.

make your own clothes. In addition, the store also sold paint, dye, linseed oil, kerosene oil, furniture, homeopathic and patent medicines and so many other things that it would take a whole page to mention them all.

When our country had a Democratic president the post office was in Hall's store, and Frank Hall carried the mail from the railroad postal car to the store. If the Republicans held power in Washington, the post office was moved to Allen's store. The post office equipment was owned by the store and kept there. It was known that when Washington changed parties, the post office would move accordingly. That was before civil service.

The railroad and all other industries paid their workers in cash. The Hall family had a small furniture factory on Hall's Island, a short distance from East Branch. They had to keep a sum of money on hand for payday. This money was kept in neat piles on a large table upstairs at the East Branch store.

Across from Hall's was another hotel and next to that was the home of Dr. Johnson, who was everyone's

family doctor. He walked to the patient's home. He attended births and deaths, and dealt with accidents, the flu, measles, and anything else except surgery. The doctor was everyone's friend, and his wife was one of three teachers in the local school.

Next to Dr. Johnson's was a small store that sold candy, school books and supplies, etc. Parents had to buy all school books and supplies. If a child had been careful with the textbook, it could be sold to a pupil promoted from a lower grade at the end of the term.

Next toward the river was Allen's store, with the big Indian weather vane on a tower above the third story. It was built by the Redman's Lodge, a secret organization that was disbanded in the late nineteenth century. The second floor was the social hall and political center. The first floor was the store, which sold much the same merchandise as Hall's, except that Allen's had an ice house, so it could sell fresh meat.

The Indian Chief weather vane on the tower of Allen's store was a symbol for the fraternal organization known as "The Improved Order of Redmen." Made of copper and painted, the weather vane dated

Hall's store in East Branch with its high tower.
Both: Marjorie Fitch Collection.

Jim Allen was the town's undertaker, and he had a beautiful horse-drawn coach with beveled glass sides so the coffin could be seen.

The last building on the same side of the street was a small, one-story millinery shop. All the ladies bought their hats there, and every lady wore a hat whenever she went out. Across the street was a blacksmith shop open to shoe horses and repair wagons. The railroad station was in the center of the town, a joint station for the D&N and the O&W and a busy place for passengers, express, and freight. It had a telegraph key for sending and receiving, not only for the railroad's business, but other important news and messages. (Even the news of FDR's death in 1945 was first heard in East Branch over that same telegraph.)

Directly across from the station was a hotel and boardinghouse where some single railroad workers lived. A little west of the boardinghouse was a small restaurant for accommodation of railroad passengers

from the mid-to late-nineteenth century. About nine feet tall, it was the largest one of its type known.

The weather vane had many holes caused by the local boys, often led by Jim Allen's son Clarence. They used to go across the river and shoot at the Indian to see if they could make it spin. It can now be found in the Museum of American Folk Art in New York City.

Members of the Redman's Lodge wore badges at their meetings and elected new members by the "black ball" ballot. The club disbanded by 1900, but no one was allowed to go to the third floor where the "Redmen" had held their meetings for as long as Jim Allen lived.

Many other societies at this time adopted Indian customs and dress. During the Revolution and the War of 1812 numerous volunteers called themselves "The Sons of Tammany." Tammany was a chief of the Delaware Indians who was revered in the early days of the Republic for his courage and eloquence.

**Allen's store in East Branch with its
9 ft. Indian weather vane.**

Railroad station and water tower at East Branch
Merlin Twaddell Collection.

who had a short layover between trains. Behind the station was the home of the town's barber—a Mr. MacDowell. His shop occupied half of the front of the building, and his wife sold ice cream cones in the other half. The ice cream was kept from melting by salted ice.

There was a drugstore, last run by S. A. Williams. The druggist mixed medicines in a back room, which was shared once a month by an itinerant dentist. The drug store also sold patent and homeopathic medicines, but the most wonderful thing about it was the soda fountain, with a marble counter and high seats that would swing around.

The town had two railroad crossings, both manned by a watchman, who had a watchman's shanty to rest in between trains. Near the southern crossing was a charcoal-drying shed, and across from that was the feed store where feed and coal were sold by the bag. Next came the three-room grade school.

Most of the towns, including East Branch, had schools for only the first eight grades, which were taught by one to three teachers. Downsville and Margaretville both had high schools where neighboring villages sent their most promising pupils. High school pupils from East Branch went to Roscoe on the O&W Mountain Express. It got them to school a little late, and they had to wait for the afternoon train, but they were able to get a high school education.

The grade schools were all run about the same way. Each school district annually elected one or more trustees to hire the teacher and be responsible for paying all bills.

Every year almost every school had an epidemic of chicken pox, measles, mumps, and sometime whooping cough, diphtheria, scarlet fever or infantile paralysis. In case of a serious contagious disease, the local doctor would put a big red sign on the front door of the sick person's home saying in big letters QUARANTINE. As long as that sign stayed on the door, nobody was supposed to leave or enter the house. Food was brought to the back door and picked up by the family later. The doctor took down the sign as soon as danger of the disease spreading was over.

Nearly every year a head lice epidemic struck the schools. The standard treatment was to wash the hair with kerosene oil and then strong soap. The hair was combed with a fine-tooth comb every day to make sure that all the lice were gone.

Sometimes the big boys would go into the woods in the spring and eat the so-called wild leeks. The odor would be so strong the next day that the teacher would send them home, and they would have a day's vacation.

Every morning the teacher read from the Bible. The students all recited the Lord's Prayer, sang songs, and said the Pledge of Allegiance.

The school Christmas party was the highlight of the year. The teacher held practice sessions with the pupils for weeks. There were recitations, elaborate plays, songs by all and solos by pretty girls wearing fancy dresses. The mothers would proudly sew costumes for the plays, each trying to outdo the others. The smallest children would sometimes be so bashful that they would just get up on the makeshift stage, hang their heads and smile. The people all clapped because the children were so cute. It gave them confidence in themselves, and was a wonderful experience. Fathers, mothers, aunts, uncles, cousins and friends all came to see the performance and loudly clapped for each and every child. That night there were more proud faces in town than at any other time. It was a night when the whole town or school district got together in peace and harmony.

Churches also had Christmas programs. The Sunday School teachers rehearsed their classes, and sometimes the same recitation was used in both church and school. It certainly lost none of its appeal the second time around. Again the whole family came to the performance, and again the children were the pride and joy of the whole family.

The Baptist Church was next to the grade school, and the Methodist Church was a short distance up the street. Both churches were well attended. In the summer there would be Free Methodist camp meetings held in tents in a wooded area. These two Methodist denominations were not connected.

Socony Oil had a branch station at East Branch where gasoline, kerosene and oil were stored in tanks before being transported from there to the nearby farms and villages. The company first used mule-drawn wagons, then later used motorized trucks. Ralph Sperbeck was one of the last mule-drivers

The East Branch Methodist Church with an open bell tower.
Both: Marjorie Fitch Collection.

The East Branch Baptist Church next to the schoolhouse.

before going on to drive the trucks. Later the Grange used the storage building, and the tanks were torn down. The Grange was a state-wide farm association that met once a month. All new information useful to farmers was read at the meetings, and the state association would personally answer any question sent to them. The parent organization held meetings all over the county to teach the farmers about new methods or equipment. Farm wives were shown new ways to cook or can food, to sew the present fashions in clothing, or how to make a mattress or quilt.

There was an excelsior mill and a foundry down the tracks from Hall's store. The foundry made commercial castings and also castings for broken farm machinery or stove grates, while the excelsior mill shredded wood for packing around fragile things. There was no plastic foam in those days.

The sawmill was located by the river near where the D&N crossed old Route 17. Jim Hubbell owned the mill, and after the arrival of the railroads he had a much wider market for his lumber.

Judge Mallory lived next to the White Building. He was Justice of the Peace and had power from the state

Jim Hubbell's saw mill was just below the D&E tracks at East Branch.
Marjorie Fitch Collection.

to perform marriages, with a charge of 50 cents. Most people paid him, but one time the groom asked how much he owed. When told "the state allows me 50 cents," he replied, "Well if the state pays you 50 cents to get me hitched, that ought to be enough," and left without paying anything.

Social Life in a Small Town

Churches were at the center of social life in the small villages in the 1870-1920 era. Anyone who did not go to church rather regularly was not respected and missed out on lots of activities. There was church and Sunday School on Sunday, at least once during the day, and a midweek prayer meeting held at various homes. Women of the church gathered at least once a month for the Ladies Aid meetings. There they sewed clothing to send to the missionaries or give to a poor family in town, so that the children would have decent clothing for school and church. Sometimes they would make a quilt to be auctioned off or sew things to be sold at a bazaar. In times of war, they knitted sweaters and such to be sent to the soldiers. This was their monthly visit with each other for talks of local happenings, and gossip or discussion of their illnesses.

There were various ways to raise money for the church. Only the "suppers" and the bazaars put on by the ladies of the church still survive. Easy transportation, television, better communication and more money available to spend have changed the way people amuse themselves.

Churchgoers used to have "box socials" to raise money for the church and have a little fun. Each of the ladies would pack a box lunch for two and decorate it to be as attractive as possible. The name of the maker of the box was supposed to be a secret, but sometimes a lady would "leak out" what her box looked like. Sometimes false information would be whispered about the room.

When the big night arrived, the ladies gathered on one side of the room with the gentlemen on the opposite side. An auctioneer stood in front of the room where the boxes were stacked. The name of the lady who packed the lunch was sealed inside her box, and only announced by the auctioneer after the gentleman had paid for the box. The boxes were auctioned off one by one, and the bidding was very brisk on some— slower on others. The lucky bidder got to eat his lunch with his lady and spend some time talking to her. No cheating by means of trading partners was allowed. This kind of auction was very popular with the young people, as you can imagine.

Another way of pairing off for the evening was by bidding on a shoe. Again the men were on one side of the room and the ladies on the other, but this time they were separated by a large white sheet. A lady would show just the tip of her shoe under the bottom of the sheet. The man would bid in hopes of getting a chance to spend the evening with the lady of his choice. However, there was no rule that the lady had to wear her own shoe, and there was much conspiracy and giggling as the women tried to fool the men.

A similar arrangement was "shadow bidding." Again a sheet separated the two sexes. The women stood in back of the sheet with a rather dim light behind them. (This was before electricity came to the area.) The men would bid on the shadow appearing on the sheet. The lady could assume any pose: stand on a box to appear taller, stoop down to appear shorter, turn sideways or put on funny clothes, like a big hat or big long coat. You can safely bet that many a lady told her favorite beau how to be sure he was bidding on the right shadow.

Every summer Chautauqua came to town for about three days. This was a cultural show, held in Allen's Hall, and was looked forward to all year long. A lot of entertainment and education was crowded into those afternoon and evening shows, and the discussions about all the wonders lasted until the next summer. There were lectures on many subjects, magic lantern (slide) shows, amateur shows, charcoal-picture drawing exhibits, plays, music, bird shows (cockatoo putting out a fire, etc.), sewing lessons and many other interesting subjects. You could buy a season ticket or a ticket for just one show. These shows faded away in the late 1920s.

In almost all the towns there was a town hall. Dances were held there about once a week, and music was commonly provided by a small group, perhaps a piano and fiddle, or maybe just a piano. A caller was needed for square dances. There were both round and square dances every time. In some towns musicians played more square dances than waltzes; it all depended on local preferences. Some of the church people frowned on these dances.

Political rallies, voting in the fall, and other important public meetings were held in the town hall.

In some town halls silent-movie shows were given. Folding chairs were put up, a large white sheet was stretched across the wall in front, and, with someone to play the piano, they were all set. The pianist would play all through the movie while she watched. She would play fast time during an exciting scene, slow for sad parts, and a love song during the romantic scenes. Sometimes it was hard to wait for the captions to appear on the screen explaining what had been said. You could always tell a simple "yes" or "no" but more complicated conversations were difficult. By the time "talkies" appeared, the family car was available to take the family to a nearby larger town to see the movies in a real movie theater.

There were traveling "medicine shows" that moved from town to town and seldom stayed in one place more than one day and night. They often traveled in several wagons, drawn by horses. One of the wagons would open up to form a platform where the entertainment appeared anytime a crowd showed up. There were different shows every time. They might have dancing girls, or performing animals, and sometimes a fortune teller. Always their "medicine" was guaranteed to cure any ailment of man or beast.

Often in the summer a circus came to town. They would set up the big tent in a large field, have a parade all through town about noon and then have one show that afternoon and one in the evening. There would be big colorful posters up for two weeks before the circus arrived. Everyone was waiting for the big day when they got to see elephants, tigers, bears, dancing dogs, performing ponies and monkeys, and all sorts of wonderful things. Sometimes if your folks couldn't afford to let you go, the circus would let you do work for a free ticket, and sometimes kids just tried to lift the bottom of the tent enough to see under it and view the circus for free. Of course this was never a big circus, but as it was the only circus most folks ever saw, it greatly fascinated the local people.

In the summer, the Free Methodists held tent meetings in various groves around the countryside. People from all around drove or walked to the meetings, getting there early to meet old friends and acquaintances. In the evenings, the glow of the torchlight illuminated the tree-shadowed grounds. Many were the boys and girls that came hoping for a chance to slip through the trees and steal a kiss. There were several small tents for the preacher and his followers to live in. The big main tent was set up with wooden benches; a path ran down the center, covered by sawdust, which led to a raised wooden platform. The itinerant preachers needed no sound system to make themselves heard. They preached vigorously against jewelry (even wedding rings), card playing, dancing, short hair or short skirts for women, drinking, smoking, holding hands in public, etc. Everyone joined loudly in singing the hymns of praise and many eagerly accepted the invitation to come forward and be saved. Theirs was a very strict and solemn religion. Sometimes some of the town's girls would get dressed in their shortest skirts, wear all the jewelry that they owned, and sit up front where they could be seen. They were wisely ignored and went home disappointed. Many heavy drinkers repented annually when the tent meeting was in town, but backslid as soon as the preacher moved on.

This was a time in the life of our country when neighbors were really neighbors in the true sense of the word. Almost everyone was willing to help a neighbor in need of a helping hand, working hard to get the work done, but also enjoying the company and companionship of friends at the same time. Since most folks worked alone on their own farms every day, a chance to talk with someone outside of the family was always welcome.

There were corn-husking bees when people all gathered at someone's home for lots of fun and incidentally to get the corn ready for drying. Quilting bees were popular in the fall after the harvest was in. Barn raisings were a time for hard work and visiting. If a farmer needed a new barn to replace one that had burned down, or to take care of more cattle or for any other reason, all his neighbors gathered for the day, and by night the barn was finished or nearly finished. The men built the barn, and the women cooked all the food for that big gathering. Members of the community would travel to the farm of a sick neighbor to gather his crops for him. They knew that if any of them needed help at any time, the neighbors would run to their aid. The unfortunate side of having such close association was that there was little privacy, and what one neighbor didn't know about another could be easily supplied by imagination. Real or suspected wrongdoings were topics of conversation for a long period of time in an area where fresh news was scarce.

The Walton Fair was the highlight of the year. That came in the early fall, after most of the harvest was in. All the ladies baked their best food and brought their finest pickles and preserved foods to be judged. Competition was intense, and many went home vowing to be the winner next year. The men brought their best livestock to be judged, and again the competition was strong. Some of the men would sleep next to their livestock to be sure nothing happened to the cow, pig, chicken, or horse. There were contests to determine which team of horses could pull the heaviest loads, a tug of war to determine which team was the strongest, and races to pick the fastest horse. Many farm families had a hired man to help with the heavy work on the farm. This was often someone who wasn't too bright, or who, for some other reason, couldn't get any other job. The hired man usually worked for room and board and a little pocket money and was generally treated as one of the family. At Walton Fair time, the farm family stayed and camped out during the whole fair, leaving the hired man home to take care of what remained home on the farm. Sometimes he came during the day and went back home to do the chores at night. There was other entertainment at the fair, but it was much more farm-oriented in the old days than it is now.

Probably all this sounds dull and boring to today's people, but back in those times folks were happy and contented with these simple pleasures. Busy with their everyday chores, they didn't have time to be bored, so they really appreciated whatever entertainment came their way.

The old fire alarm at East Branch was made from a steam engine tire and pieces of railroad rail. The rail bed has been converted to a county road.

The acid factory at Corbett.
Edward P. Baumgardner Collection.

Chapter 4
BUSINESSES ALONG THE RAILS

Acid Factories

There never was much originating freight on this little railroad, and for much of the life of the D&N the acid factories produced most of it. The plant at Corbett, built in 1912, was the largest acid factory ever constructed, and it could never have operated on such a large scale without convenient rail transportation. The acid-factory business was located in a rather small section of the country, producing wood alcohol and acetate of lime and charcoal.

The Centerville factory and the one at Harvard were owned by Corbett and Stuart. The Harvard factory, built about 1890, shut down around 1910. Corbett and Stuart then built the big factory at Corbett, closing the Centerville operation when the new factory opened. The plant up the brook at Shinhopple was owned by L. B. Corbett, a nephew of Corbett's, and run by Nick Erst. It was built by Mr. Finch.

There were also acid factories at Shavertown and Arkville. One at Shavertown was built about 1916-17

Trout Brook at Shinhopple near acid factory.

Shinhopple acid factory was located up Shinhopple Brook. Chet Fitch is standing holding a baby and Roma Fitch is next to him.

Both: Marjorie Fitch Collection

by George Merritt, a lumberman, and his brother, Decker Merritt. That shut down shortly after World War I.

At Centerville there was no railroad station. It was a flag stop. (At a flag stop one stood along the tracks and waved for the engineer to stop.) There was no station to wait in. However there was an acid factory across the river and up the brook a little way. It was important to get the products from the factory at Centerville to the railroad. A narrow-gauge track was laid across a suspension bridge and cars loaded with drums of alcohol, acetate of lime and charcoal were pulled up to the D&E by a steam winch. The empty cars were returned to the plant by gravity. This track was built by the acid factory, and the railroad put in a siding for the factory's use. The railroad was always glad to put in a siding to accommodate a good customer.

Archie Williams, the winch operator, nearly lost his whole arm when his coat sleeve was caught in the gears. It pulled his arm and chewed it all the way up to his shoulder before it could be stopped. Hannah Malloch Rosenstraus, who lives along the Delaware River near there, was at home when the accident happened. She says she could hear the agonizing scream at her place and she will never forget that scream. Archie was crippled for the rest of his life, but as soon as he was able, he was given a job that it was possible for him to do with only one arm, and the acid factory kept him on the payroll. That was the way responsible employers took care of any employee who was injured on the job.

Besides the actual acid factory, there were other support activities and jobs. There had to be horse barns, blacksmith and carpentry shops, and a sawmill to saw up all those big logs. Some of the lumber from the sawmill was sold to the railroad for ties and for building boxcars. The more valuable woods such as cherry, maple, and white pine were shipped to furniture factories. Many farmers earned a little extra money in the winter, by cutting logs from their own timberland and drawing it to the acid factory nearest them.

A cutter working for the acid factory was paid 80 cents per cord of wood cut. A cord of wood measured four feet by four feet by eight feet.

The factory needed a large acreage of timberland and this was acquired nearby. Most was purchased outright. In many cases the factories failed to pay taxes on their timberland, letting it be sold for back taxes after all the wood was cut. Other land was leased, or the wood was cut on a royalty basis for so-much-per-cord of wood cut on the tract with the title to the property (and the liability for taxes) retained by the owner.

Mostly the factories had their own teams and men to haul out the wood. Each man had his own company team and rigging that he took care of. The man and horses usually became quite attached to each other. In the winter, sleds replaced wagons, and the operation continued. Oxen were used to get wood from the steepest places. When the acid factories had used all the hard wood from the nearby mountains, wood was shipped in by rail to fill the need.

Acid factories were operated 24 hours a day, seven days a week. The men worked 12-hour shifts for $1.60 a day.

Each factory had a big steam whistle which was blown exactly at noon every day. Everyone for miles around timed their midday meal and other activities by this whistle.

In Corbett there were three miles of track within the factory complex and the factory had a small Shay to do its own switching. The railroad ran a telegraph line into the company office, where a young man named Ray Woodin, the company bookkeeper, learned telegraphy. He was then appointed agent for the railroad, and in 1912 the office became the railroad station, post office, and company general store. Woodin became the postmaster for Corbett, N. Y., in addition to his other duties. Later at Corbett there was a ticket agent by the name of Fred Lewis, who was the fastest telegrapher in the business. He could send and receive at the same time.

During World War I, the railroad was under orders to move the acetate of lime produced by the acid factories in preference to any other freight. Traffic in and out of the acid factories on the D&N averaged about six carloads a day during the war, a substantial amount for a small railroad. Acetate of lime was used in the manufacturing of smokeless gunpowder, and as a solvent for the paint used on the fabric outer-covering of airplanes. Production at Corbett equaled the combined production of all the other acid factories along the D&N.

Most charcoal was sold to the steel mills to harden steel. Some was sold to burn in kitchen stoves in the summer, as it did not heat up the kitchen as much as coal or wood.

Wood alcohol was used in the early automobiles as antifreeze.

The acetic acid derived from the acetate of lime was used extensively in the dyes made then. The Germans developed a synthetic chemical to use in place of acetic acid and wood alcohol during World War I, and this was the main reason that the acid factory business faded away after the war over a period of only a few years.

Acid factories were dirty, smelly places to work in. However, if you worked in one, all your needs were met by the Company. They built houses and rented them to the workers, as well as a school house, which doubled as church on Sundays. They built a company store, and sold everything that their workers needed, from food to clothes to patent medicines or hardware. Everything could be purchased on time, and by payday at the end of the month, the store got most of the worker's paycheck.

These men worked very hard at a difficult and dangerous job, but most of them would not have exchanged their security for any other job available.

After World War I, one-by-one these factories closed down forever. That was a hard blow to our railroad. The Corbett plant did operate from 1912 until 1934. It might have lasted a few years longer, except for a disagreement with the government over some provision in the National Recovery Act (NRA). After long and fruitless legal maneuvering, on February 8, 1934 the owners closed down the plant, and that night the temperature went down to about 40 degrees below zero. All the machinery with pipes and coils full of water froze and ruptured, despite efforts to keep the plant warm without the heat generated by machines operating. The factory was dismantled for its junk value, throwing its workers out of their jobs at the height of the Depression. The village of Corbett lost its only employer and its economic base.

That was the last acid factory on the D&N and the last bit of originating freight on the whole road. In many places, after the factory shut down, all the people moved away and the houses were left to fall down. Then nature took over and soon it was hard to locate the community. Berry bushes grew wild, then trees grew, and it was once again a wilderness.

Top photo: Stanley Horton Collection.
Middle photo: L&L Photos Collection.
Bottom photo by Stanley Horton.

Corbett & Stuart's Shay, about 1910, when nearly new. It was never owned by the D&N. The initials were added to the photo later.

Corbett and Stuart's old Shay #3 in 1936 after the factory was closed. It has a rebuilt wooden cab and a hot water tank for a smoke stack.

The Corbett general store, post office, and D&N station in 1974.

Creameries

Before the railroad, the only way for the farmers to sell their surplus milk was to make butter. The farmers would "dry up" most of their cows in the winter and plan to have them freshen in the spring. There had been one creamery at Shavertown before the railroad, but that only made butter and cheese.

The railroad built its own creameries; in some places the creameries were put up even before the station. The railroad also had ice ponds where 100,000 tons of ice were harvested every winter in about three weeks time. January and February were the best months for filling the ice houses as the thickness of the ice was maximum in those months and the frigid air

allowed trainloads to be moved or to sit on a siding without fear of melting. The main source of ice was a 17-acre pond located near Muir's trestle. There were other ice ponds; one was located near Downsville.

Icing was the only way to keep the milk from all those farmers fresh and cold enough to reach New York City in good condition. Half of each creamery was an ice house where tons of ice were stored. The other half was for weighing, straining, cooling and storing the milk until time for shipment. The farmer was paid according to the percentage of butterfat in the milk. If he had a Jersey herd the butterfat content was higher than for Holstein cows, so he got more per

Engine #3 at the Downsville creamery. Note the pile of milk cans on the creamery platform.
John Ham Collection.

Creamery at Pepacton.
Merlin Twaddell Collection.

Milk cans on the D&E platform at Downsville.
Marjorie Fitch Collection.

Milk cans on a flat car at the Dunraven station.
E. P. Baumgardner Collection.

D&E Engine #2 and a milk wagon on the Andes branch.
Edward P. Baumgardner Collection.

gallon. By paying according to fat content the creameries were able to discourage watering the milk.

Being able to ship fresh fluid milk to the big city markets was a profitable change for the local people. The farmer brought the milk to the creamery by nine o'clock in the morning. That meant getting up at about four o'clock A.M. He and his family had to milk the cows and cool the milk. Then he ate breakfast and drove his horses with a wagon full of milk cans to the railroad creamery.

Sometimes the farmer would be so tired by then that he would let the reins go slack, allowing the horse to find its way home while the farmer got a little much-needed rest. Most farmers lived on roads without much other traffic, and no cars. The horse knew its way home as well as the farmer did.

In some places, one farmer would take the job of hauling all the milk for neighboring farms to the creamery. Then each farmer only had to haul his own milk to a central pick-up place.

The milk trains were the only trains, other than passenger trains, that were held to a schedule on the D&N. Even passenger trains had to move onto a siding to let the milk trains pass so they could meet the New York bound O&W milk trains on time. This arrangement lasted only a few years until big tank trucks took over the profitable milk business from the railroads.

At Margaretville, the D&E creamery became the general office for the D&N. Mr. Jordan built another creamery at Margaretville, which was sold first to Hosea Barnhart, a local merchant, and Arthur Brundage and was called the B&B Creamery. Later it was taken over by the Dairymen's League. At Arena the D&E's creamery was sold to the Arena Creamery Company. At Shavertown the D&E built a new creamery to replace the old Hulbert Creamery, which became the Whittaker dance hall and movie theater. In 1920 a group started the Dan Franklin Creamery (near Shavertown), and the railroad creamery became a plant to make excelsior from poplar trees. Later the Dan Franklin Creamery was affiliated with the Dairymen's League. The Pepacton Creamery was leased to Borden Milk Company and later purchased by the B&B Creamery. At Downsville the creamery was sold to Breakstone Brothers. On the Andes branch, after several years of use, the railroad's creamery was used for storage and the old school-house on the Tremperskill became the Andes Creamery Company. That burned down in 1921 and was rebuilt with modern machinery. Again in 1929 fire destroyed it, and this time it was not rebuilt. In 1915 a different creamery was built in Andes called the Andes Cooperative Creamery. It burned down in 1952 and a more modern plant was built to replace it.

Providing ice to be used in the creameries involved a lot of work and expense for the railroad. This was the main reason why they got out of the creamery business, leaving it up to private operators to worry about getting their own ice. The railroad was satisfied just to get the business of hauling the finished product.

A New Use for an Old Creamery

By 1924 the old railroad creamery in Andes had been boarded up, and since no one else seemed to have any use for it, some of the railroad men decided to make good, although illegal, use of this building.

Down in the cool dark depths of the creamery was a very good place to make wine. The country was dry, the men were thirsty, and they could not afford the price charged by the local bootlegger. An Italian section-foreman had the necessary skills and led the highly successful enterprise. This operation went on for quite some time, but finally the sheriff heard a whisper about some good wine being produced there. The sheriff's department staged a big raid, and the men had to locate a new place for their wine making.

The Teeth of the Evidence

Cheese, as well as other dairy products, was shipped from the creameries to New York City by rail. One time a group of hungry workers broke into a shipment of cheese and ate some of it. The culprits left a half-eaten chunk, and when it was found, one of them was identified by the marks left by his crooked teeth in the cheese. (Told by Mel Fingado.)

The Bluestone Business

Farmers in the area had always supplemented their income by cutting bluestone in the winter months when farm work was slow. Now there was a way to get their stone to the profitable city markets. Before the railroad was constructed, the quarry stone had to be hauled all the way to either East Branch and the Ontario & Western Railroad or to Arkville and the Ulster & Delaware Railroad. Since a horse and wagon or sled was the only means of transportation, it was a slow and difficult way to get the stone to market.

There was no way to quarry enough stone to satify the demand for this beautiful and useful sandstone. Bluestone was used for sidewalks, curbing, buildings and walls. Bluestone is not really blue. It is more of a blue-gray and can vary in color from quarry to quarry, sometimes displaying an almost green-gray color.

Deposits of the stone appear in horizonal layers of uniform thickness, but the thickness also varies from quarry to quarry. The farmer would uncover the stone, pry loose the layer with wedges, and if he was skillful he could pry up the stone layer by layer. Sometimes two or three men would need to work together on some of the harder, heavier layers. These farmers were used to helping each other, and thought nothing of delaying their own work to help a neighbor.

Almost every station had a stone dock where all the stonecutters could bring their stone for shipping to the welcoming markets. Transportation to the docks was usually by horse and sled, since most of the stonecutting was done in the winter. Of course this was not a big profit industry for the railroad, but every little bit helped.

Under a joint agreement with the D&E/D&N and the O&W, the cost for carload lots of bluestone from any point on the D&N to Weehawken and Brooklyn was $2.50 per ton. Less than carload lots cost more per ton. The road originating the freight always got more than connecting roads, so this was good for the D&E/D&N.

Johnston and Rhodes still has a large stone dock at East Branch, but now all transporting is done by huge trucks. Companies today have modern equipment, and complicated shapes can be cut, using diamond saws.

Bluestone is highly prized as an architectural addition to many modern buildings. Concrete is now used for sidewalks but can never replace the beautiful bluestone for any decorative construction work.

Two views of the bluestone dock at Shinhopple. Note: there are two trains in the picture above.
Edward P. Baumgardner Collection.

Marjorie Fitch Collection.

Building the Gerry Estate

For a little over a year the building of a summer home for Robert L. Gerry, a New York City financier, gave the D&N quite a lot of business. His new home was located at Lake Delaware, about four miles northwest of Andes on the Gerry estate—a vast acreage of fertile farmland which had been part of the old Livingston Patent. (Patents were huge land grants, sometimes almost two million acres, made by the colonial governors. Later these tracts were broken up and sold.)

Robert's brother, Senator Elbridge Gerry of Rhode Island, and his sister, Angelica Gerry of New York City, already had summer homes here. Each brother or sister had been assigned a section of the estate, and their homes resembled the architectural style of the old English manors.

This area was the only one in this part of the country to be scientifically farmed. Each farm was stocked with registered cows and horses, and rare fruits, vegetables and grains were grown experimentally. A large game preserve was established around a natural lake for the propagation of wild ducks, pheasants, and grouse.

The Gerry families furnished employment for many local people; a majority of the workers and their families lived in tenant houses located on the estate.

Robert's mansion was constructed to be as near fireproof as possible, with a steel frame, concrete sidewalls, asphalt waterproofing, and brick and gypsum blocks. It had 40 rooms and was said to cost $2 million. Gerry also built large barns for his show horses, polo ponies and wagons, besides all the other outbuildings. Carloads of fine show horses and polo ponies were moved in and out. Often Robert Gerry chartered a special train to bring himself and his family from Andes to Arkville, then on to New York City via the Ulster & Delaware and West Shore Railroads.

All material used in the construction of this estate was transported by the Delaware & Northern Railroad, then brought to the building site by horse-drawn wagons and small trucks. There was a large work force of both skilled and unskilled laborers, and all the groceries, work clothes, and other supplies came in on the D&N for the commissary owned by Nick Farone and managed by Jerry Lauro.

The town of Andes had been dry for years, and still was, but shipments of 40 or 50 half barrels of beer ar-rived regularly on the D&N for the men working on Gerry's estate. One day there was a shipment of beer at the freight house waiting to be picked up. The sheriff came through the freight house to see who the beer was addressed to, but there was only an L on the kegs. He demanded to know who the beer was for, but the station agent said the only way he could release such information would be if the sheriff got a court order.

The next morning the local delivery man came to pick up the kegs and was warned by the station agent that there might be a raid on the camp that day. In spite of the warning the delivery man loaded some of the beer kegs on the wagon and started for the workers' camp. He had gone only a little way when he was met by a messenger from the camp and told to return the beer to the station. The sheriff had already been at the camp that morning and was expected back any time. A couple of days later the beer was moved to the job and no further raids were conducted.

The estate was finished in early April of 1913, and the owner of the commissary, Nick Farone (who had made money on all the sales to the laborers), decided to give a big dance with refreshments for the townspeople, to show appreciation for their cooperation and assistance. A big-name dance band from Albany—Zito's Orchestra—was hired to furnish the music.

All the invited guests and help had arrived by nine o'clock that evening, but there was no sign of the orchestra. Tracing them by many different telephone calls disclosed that they had somehow left their train at the wrong station and they were now at Bloomville.

Farone was determined not to disappoint all his guests, so he started for Bloomville in his big seven-passenger Pope-Toledo car. All the roads in the area were dirt roads and were knee-deep in soft spring mud. Before leaving Andes Farone phoned the orchestra and instructed them to hire a team of horses and start for Delhi. He would meet them on the way. At Delhi he phoned the commissary and asked them for a second car to be sent to Delhi just in case he got hopelessly stuck in the mud. Farone did indeed get stuck halfway between Delhi and Bloomville, but the second car got through and saved the party.

The orchestra arrived at 12:30 A.M., and everyone was still waiting. The program called for 20 numbers, and with only a short intermission at three o'clock, the 20 numbers had been played by seven o'clock the next morning.

The dancers left for their homes, and the orchestra left for the hotel and some sleep. Farone went off with several men to dig his Pope-Toledo out of the mud. The Gerry estate gave the D&N a lot of business for about a year, and that helped.

The estate of Robert Gerry at Lake Delaware between Andes and Delhi, New York.
Bernard Wadler Collection.

Movies Made on the D&N

Through the Snow

Two movies were made on the Andes branch of the D&N. Muir's trestle, two miles below Andes, was featured during the winter of 1913-14 in a movie using D&N equipment. The name of the movie was *Through the Snow*—and that winter produced plenty of snow. Two actors were seen running back and forth across the swaying boxcars, just ahead of the passenger coach, as the train crossed Muir's trestle. They were fighting over a beautiful girl who was riding in the coach below. Of course, the good guy won and the bad guy fell off the train. Not much is now known of this picture, except that all the railroaders were surprised that actors would dare run along the tops of the cars when the train was crossing Muir's trestle.

The Single Track

In the summer of 1920, Vitagraph Motion Picture Company—a leader in motion picture production—was looking for a place to photograph a movie about a mining and lumbering railroad in Alaska. As Vitagraph didn't want the expense and inconvenience of taking their actors and equipment all the way to Alaska, the movie scouts found the locale of the D&N to have just the right setting. Soon Margaretville was invaded by actors, actresses, camera crews and many assistants. Lots of local people dreamed of being "discovered" and becoming famous. Pocantico Inn was the headquarters of the movie company, and the Inn enjoyed all the extra business.

This movie, named *The Single Track*, was based on a popular book of that title. The star was the great silent-screen actress, Corrine Griffith, considered to be one of the most beautiful women of the silent era. In her spare time she enjoyed trout fishing along the Delaware River at Margaretville.

Included in the movie were many scenes typical of those found in the railroad movies popular at that time such as men racing along the tracks and escaping in a locomotive that happened to be handy, and a raft being blown up in the river alongside the train.

The main scene called for rival gangs to race along the tracks and meet in the middle of Moore's trestle—the longer Muir's trestle had been filled by this time, and was no longer photogenic. Vitagraph planned to use a lot of local people for the two gangs. As it happened, there were hard feelings in the area between two groups of local men, due to quarrels about who cheated whom in a cow and horse trade. There were even more hard feelings about someone accusing someone else of stealing wood and chickens. Here was a wonderful chance to spot an enemy in the opposite gang and legally get even. The locals would have done this scene even if they hadn't been paid for it, and the movie company got some really good shots of the two gangs fighting on the trestle. Vitagraph never had to shoot a retake, and they were heard to remark how real the "battle" appeared. Many of the wooden props and even the camera platforms were broken up to make clubs for the eager new "actors," and the innocent movie company had a difficult time trying to stop the fight.

The hero was supposed to jump off the trestle in the height of the battle and be caught in a net out of sight of the camera. He didn't want to take the risk, and someone else had to be found to do that scene. Next, a few mannequins were dumped over the side of the trestle, and the big splash into the water of the Tremperskill was recorded on camera.

The mannequins caused some excitement when, years later, they were found in an unused dark storage area and mistaken for real bodies. The cry of mass murder was soon stilled when a little light was shone on the scene, but the poor man who had discovered the "bodies" took a few days to get over his fright.

The premier showing was in the old opera house at Margaretville. All the local people wanted to see themselves or friends in this movie, and the size of the crowds caused the movie to be shown for several nights. If only it had been that popular elsewhere, it might have been saved, although the review in *Variety* said it contained enough "meller thrills" to please any audience.

The Single Track was a silent movie with subtitles and was destroyed when Warner Brothers took over Vitagraph in the late 1920s.

The most important consequence for the railroad of being a movie location was that a problem the road had with the state inspector was temporarily solved. He had been threatening to shut down the trestle if some much needed repairs weren't done. The movie company sprayed the old hemlock timbers with a mixture of clay and water to make them more photogenic. The next time the bridge inspector came around, he was very pleased: he remarked that the railroad had finally taken his advice, made the necessary repairs and, in fact, had done more than he had required. The local people had a good laugh at his expense, since no actual repairs had been made.

It was mentioned earlier that there had been some hard feelings about stealing wood. This was quite common practice among the population at that time. It wasn't that they were so dishonest; they just "borrowed" a few sticks when their own supply got low. Families all burned wood in both the kitchen and heating stoves. After you borrowed a few sticks, you could always return some when you got your next load. Of course, you would have to do it at night when the neighbor couldn't see you. Also, you would have to be careful there wasn't fresh snow so that your tracks didn't lead back to your kitchen door in the morning. With all this difficulty not much wood was ever returned.

It got so that when someone's wood pile started disappearing too fast, that person would just "steal it back." Then somebody got an idea: just bore a hole in one end of a stick of wood, fill it with gunpowder from a shotgun shell and plug up the hole with wax. Then all there was to do was wait for someone's stove to blow up. That way you were sure to know who had some of your wood.

The best place to live was next door to a church or schoolhouse. There was a perpetual supply of free wood, well seasoned and with no danger of an explosion.

Eventually the state legislature made it a criminal act to put gunpowder in stove wood and that ended the explosions. After all, the wood burners were all law-abiding citizens.

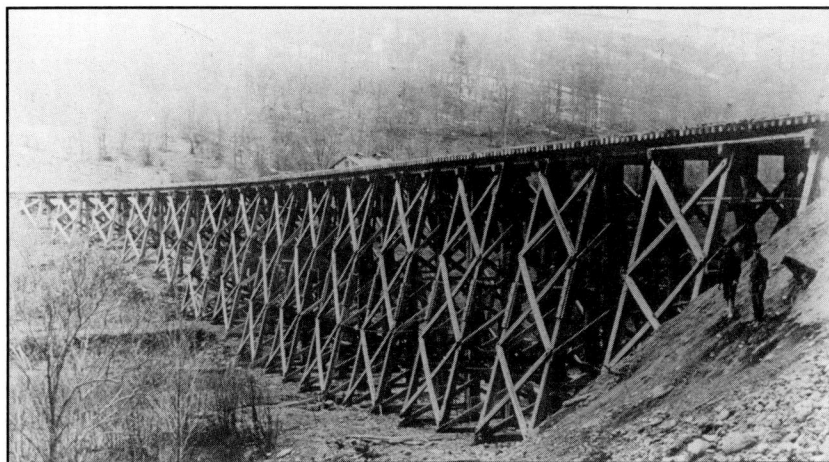

Muir's trestle where Through the Snow was filmed.
Edward P. Baumgardner Collection.

The Brill Car and a Crowley milk truck meet at East Branch.
Edward P. Baumgardner Collection.

Chapter 5
MISHAPS

Two Engines to Rescue

It was said that anything and everything that ever happened on any other railroad, no matter how big, happened on the D&N. If there had been a contest to find the most unusual happenings, I think the little D&N would have won.

One time in the early days of the road, a passenger train near Harvard developed a hotbox (a journal bearing overheated by friction) on one of the wheels of the locomotive tender. They were still trying to maintain their trains on some reasonable schedule. A young hostler named Howard Liddle was sent from Margaretville with another engine to rescue the stranded train.

The rescue engine had to back all the way. There was a 5 MPH rule about backing up an engine, as those highwheelers had a bad habit of jumping the tracks when going too fast in reverse. Liddle was told to get there as soon as possible, since the railroad wanted to keep their passengers as happy as they could. In the excitement he ignored the speed rule and surprisingly got as far as Gregorytown, going about 30 MPH in reverse, before this engine landed up against the upper bank of the tracks. Now there were two engines to rescue.

Howard was fired, which may have been unfair since he was a hostler with little experience driving a

train, but he was hired back as a trainman a year later. He was promoted to conductor and was still working at the closing of the railroad in 1942.

Locomotive in the Delaware River

A second, more serious accident was caused by the need to go many miles in reverse, coupled with the irresistible temptation to speed up and cover the territory. Before the railroad got around to installing a turntable at Andes, all the trains had to back from Andes to Arena. On May 20, 1908, as train #3 was backing into Arena from Andes, the engine jumped the track, and the tender followed it, landing in the Delaware River. The engineer, Clare Cowan, later testified that a short distance north of Union Grove the train had crossed the Jacksonville Creek bridge and he had shut off the steam and was drifting at 15 MPH. About 500 feet north of the bridge he thought the coaches derailed suddenly and the milk car turned over on its side. Whatever happened first, the result was the same. The engine was in the Delaware River.

The fireman, John Francisco, was thrown clear and made his way to the now roofless cab. He found engineer Clare Cowan face down in the water, his foot wedged by some metal part of the engine, and a part on the air pump holding him by his back. The whistle was blowing under the water as if to call for help.

Engine in the Delaware River, May 24, 1908.
William Capach Collection.

Francisco shut off the whistle and tried to help Cowan. All he could see was the back of his head under water. John felt down Cowan's back and found the lubricator to the air pump in the middle of his back. Francisco shut off the steam to the pump, very quickly broke off the lubricator holding Cowan under the water and lifted his head high enough so he could breathe.

Soon conductor Louis Sanford and some of the male passengers bent the pipe on the broken steam gauge away from the two men. That was a relief, as the steam was roaring out uncomfortably close.

The engine was resting on some very large rocks, and there was some risk that it might shift, taking engine, Cowan, and all to the deep part of the river.

Superintendent Wagenhorst directed the rescue operation. Five hours later, after careful blocking and shoring, the rescue engine, using tackle blocks with steel cables, raised the engine a few inches and freed Cowan's foot. John Francisco was there right beside him for the whole five hours, holding his head above the water and talking to him to give some encouragement to the trapped man. Francisco went to work the

next day and later said that it was the longest bath he had ever taken.

The doctor said Cowan was very lucky that he had no broken bones and no internal injuries. He didn't go back to work at once, so exhausted from the pain of his badly mashed foot and exposure to the cold water that he couldn't work again until the next autumn.

There was some talk about the 5 MPH speed limit that had been broken, and the lack of enough coal and water on the engine to make the necessary weight to hold it to the tracks. However, everyone was so glad that no one was really seriously hurt that all such talk gradually disappeared.

Very soon after that the railroad installed a turntable at Andes. Since the Andes branch was completed, the officials had been aware of the tendency of those highwheelers to climb the rails when backing up, and of the tender's ability to bounce off the rails and take the whole train with it. For over a year they just had not gotten around to remedying the problem. It was too bad it had to take such an accident to force the railroad to act.

Locomotive Tug of War

There was much excitement in East Branch in the summer of 1908. The railroad was slow in paying its property tax ($700) to the town of Hancock. Deputies from the town decided to force the issue by placing a levy on one of the road's engines. This had to be done in the town of Hancock, so it was decided to attach and hold the engine in East Branch.

The deputies knew that an engine tied up there every night. Roma Fitch was the hostler (note the use of horse-handling terms when speaking of the "iron horse" at the turn of the century). As the men approached, he thought they were just coming to visit, since often some of Roma's friends would drop in. It was always a long night, and company was welcome. However, the deputies were not in a friendly frame of mind. When Roma objected to leaving his post, they showed him the legal papers and gave him the choice of going peaceably or being bodily thrown off the engine. He asked them not to let the engine (#1) go dry or let any harm come to it. Constable Bullis, a former

Delaware & Eastern engineer (who had been fired), gave such assurances, and Roma Fitch left.

There was no telephone that he could use, and the telegraph office was closed until morning. Even if he could have persuaded someone to come to the station and use the telegraph key, there was no one in the office at Margaretville to receive the message.

The deputies chained the drive wheels to the track with heavy logging chain and waited. When the railroad crew came to work on that Saturday morning, they were met by the deputies armed with a gun and a shovel. The trainmen hastily retreated to the station and telegraphed the office at Margaretville. They were told to do nothing, but to be available when needed.

There was some excitement when a lone engine appeared, but that engine just picked up the load ready to go that morning.

Not knowing what the railroad was up to made the deputies very nervous. Nothing happened in East Branch all that day, but in Margaretville things were moving at a frantic pace. Engine #3 was the line's best engine, and it was put in the shop and given a quick

D&E Engine #1 — the engine held by the deputies.
William Capach Collection.

D&E Engine #3—the rescue engine.
William Capach Collection.

overhaul, to be sure it was in the best of condition. The deputies kept up the steam on #1 and waited for the next move from the railroad. Conditions were tense on #1, as the deputies did not know what to expect.

About noon on Sunday a whistle was heard from up Harvard way, and the townspeople gathered around to watch what would happen. With so many people around, the deputies did not dare to show their guns. There were about 15 men on the railroad's side led by superintendent Wagenhorst, all experienced men, and they knew that #3 could outpull any other engine on the pike. The railroad men quickly piled off their engine, broke the padlocks and chains on #1, and chained the two engines together, pilot to pilot. Putting #3 in reverse, they started to pull #1 up the tracks.

Constable Bullis, leading the deputies, applied the brakes to #1 and slid the wheels, and on the wye the chain broke. When the railroad men got out to fix it, a fist fight broke out. There was much confusion, smoke, steam, men swearing, and threats of bodily harm.

One of the company men somehow obtained the link pin for the chain, fastened the two engines together, and the tug of war was on again. This time the overexertion of #3 caused a loss of steam pressure. Bullis, proving to be an expert at the throttle, dragged #3 back to the starting point.

Both engines got ready for the next big pulling contest. This time #3 began dragging #1 back out of town as before, but Bullis, with the drive wheels working in reverse, got the upper hand again. Once more there was lots of smoke and steam from both engines.

John Francisco, the fireman who had rescued Clare Cowan, sneaked back under cover of the smoke and steam and, with a large pipe wrench, unscrewed the relief valves from the fronts of the steam chests on the captive engine. Steam roared out of the holes in #1's steam chests, and now #3 had undisputed control, with the tug of war at an end. Bullis and the other deputies knew the battle was lost, so they jumped off before the engines got going very fast. The railroad men never let up on the steam until they were past the Town of Hancock's boundary line.

Near Shinhopple they checked both engines, dropped the fire on #1 and proceeded triumphantly to Margaretville.

Both engines were put in the shop for an overhaul. There was very little wrong. Another engine was sent to East Branch, so Monday's freight train pulled out on time from East Branch, but old #1 did not appear there for a few days.

There were suits and countersuits. Bullis was arrested on charges of assault and threatening to use his gun. He was soon out on bail, and superintendent Wagenhorst and several of his men were arrested on a charge of riot.

The tax collector realized that the cost of trying all those men might amount to more than the taxes due, so no one was actually prosecuted. In time the railroad paid the taxes, and #1 could again safely enter East Branch.

The Door Crasher

Engine #10 seemed to have a liking for going through shop doors when the doors were closed, and even doing it against the direction of swing. In the early 30s, a young hostler backed up into the shop and forgot to open the doors. Another time someone left a switch thrown for the wrong track and Clare Cowan, driving the Brill Car, rammed poor #10 backwards through the doors again. The cab was damaged both times, and it looked worn and battered, but it was still their best locomotive.

D&E Engine #2 in the ditch south of Corbett. The derailment was caused by too much speed in reverse.
John Ham Collection.

The Chestnut Log

Many of the railroad ties were made of locally-cut chestnut. Logs not big enough to make ties for the main line could be used for the narrower ties on the sidings, which didn't have to take the heavy pounding of the main lines.

One day a group of men were cutting chestnut for ties just above Harvard. They had just finished trimming the last branches from a log and were ready to hitch it to a horse to be dragged out of the woods, when the log got away from them, rolled down a steep bank, and landed on the railroad track. The heavy log had gathered such momentum that the impact pushed the track out of line. The loggers had to rush to the station at Harvard so the agent could telegraph ahead and warn the next scheduled train not to proceed. The section gang made the necessary repairs, and traffic soon resumed. (Mel Fingado told this story.)

Horse on its Knees

Sometimes, in order to keep the tracks level, quite a high fill had to be made across a farmer's field, and he would need a way to get his cattle from one side of the right of way to the other. This was the kind of thing which had been negotiated between each farmer and the railroad before right-of-way agreements were signed. In some cases the best answer was for the railroad to build a culvert under the tracks for the cattle to pass through. Such a cattle culvert was built on Mel Fingado's farm; it was just high enough for the cattle to pass through.

This worked fine until one day when one of the big farm horses tried to go through the culvert. He almost made it, but got stuck near the far end. The poor horse had to get down on his knees, and the men pulled him through.

Army Worms

One year there was a very heavy infestation of army worms. They nearly denuded most of the trees on the nearby mountains. These worms also caused the railroad a little trouble. Wherever the tracks ran through a wooded area, the worms dropped down on the tracks in such numbers that the tracks became very slippery as the engine drove over them. The drive wheels would spin, and the engineer would use the sanders on the engine. Some days during the worst of the infestation the engine ran out of sand before the day was over, and the sanders would have to be refilled. Of course that was not a long-term or dangerous situation.

The Disappearing Boxcar

A loaded boxcar disappeared from the view of the switching crew at Andes. The only way it could go from there was back down the way it had come. It was a steep grade all the way to Andes Junction, which was 400 feet lower in elevation than Andes.

Engineer Pattberg and conductor Gus Williams started after the boxcar with the locomotive. Williams crawled out onto the pilot of the engine so he could adjust the knuckle on the coupler. They would catch sight of the runaway car only to lose sight of it when they had to slow for a curve. There was a straight stretch of track just before the last grade into Andes Junction. Pattberg speeded up there and caught the runaway just before that last descent. It was in full view of all the people in Shavertown, but no word leaked out to headquarters at Margaretville. A long time afterwards Margaretville heard of it, but by then it was too late to do anything about it.

Drawing by Harry Archer depicts a curve on the Bloodgood farm, outside Andes near the yard limits and turntable.

Almost Meeting
Cowcatcher to Cowcatcher

During ice-harvest time the train crews worked long hours. They could not be sure of the right weather from day to day. Since the ice harvest train was an extra, they had to fit their schedule to use the track when it wasn't in use by a regularly scheduled train.

One afternoon the ice train's conductor, Gus Williams, noticed that he just had time to take a load of empty flat cars down to the pond near Muir's trestle before the afternoon passenger train was due. As the ice-harvest train approached Muir's trestle, it slowed down. Looking across the narrow valley, the trainmen saw to their horror that the passenger train had already passed the switch leading to the pond.

The two locomotives stopped within a few feet of each other, and the two conductors rushed toward each other with their trusty railroad pocket watches in their hands. Each was ready to blame the other for the near accident. It turned out that the passenger train was 15 minutes early, and that the conductor was to blame for not keeping to the schedule.

In order not to endanger his job, both men agreed not to report the incident. The passenger train then backed up far enough to let the ice train pull into the pond spur.

The passenger conductor lived too far from Andes to go home every night, so the railroad allowed him to stay in an unused caboose during the week. When he began to have noisy drinking parties in the caboose, his Andes neighbors complained to Margaretville headquarters. The main office investigated and fired him.

To get even, he reported the ice train incident to the *Downsville News*. When headquarters at Margaretville saw the article in the newspaper, they suspended poor Gus for 30 days without pay because he had not reported the incident.

Trouble with Snow and Ice

There were many times when snow and ice caused canceled trains and wrecks on this railroad. In February of 1910 there was a very heavy snow storm followed by rain and sleet. The next morning it was extremely cold, and the tracks were covered with ice. (Snow and ice had to be kept clean from the inside of the rail where the flange ran, as only a small amount of ice or snow there would derail a car. This could be an almost impossible task under storm conditions.) The early morning freight only got as far as Centerville after leaving East Branch before the entire train—locomotive, eight or ten cars and the caboose—left the rails and came to rest against the rocks in a cut. Luckily they were all still standing upright; there just weren't

D&N Caboose #31 at Margaretville on August 2, 1936. Perhaps the one used for the wild parties?
L&L Photos Collection.

D&N derrick at Margaretville on July 4, 1937.

D&N wreck train at Margaretville on August 2, 1936.
Both: L&L Photos Collection.

any rails under them. Soon after that, the passenger train left Margaretville, and it too left the track and remained upright with no damage to equipment, passengers or crew.

Whenever there was a derailment, a work (rescue) train had to be sent out from Margaretville with a derrick, block and tackle, and other heavy equipment to put the rolling stock back on the rails. So a relief train piloted by Gus Williams had to travel through the storm from Margaretville to straighten out the mess. His gang of men working with picks, shovels, and crowbars, as well as other heavy wrecking equipment, soon got the passenger train back on the track. That train was sent back to Margaretville and canceled for the day.

Now to get the freight train rescued. The relief train had to proceed very slowly, so it would not be the next one to need rescuing. Just to be on the safe side, Margaretville headquarters sent another engine and coach to join Gus Williams and his crew. Gus took the lead with the coach, and the second rescue train followed. Gus traveled very cautiously, and by late afternoon got as far as Shinhopple, where he left the coach on a siding and proceeded with just the engine. He hadn't gone more than 500 feet when his engine derailed, and he had to wait in Shinhopple for the rescue train to catch up to him.

It was several miles to the rear, and didn't join Gus and his engine until about three o'clock in the morning. The men from both trains were exhausted and nearly frozen, as the temperature had dropped to 20 degrees below zero. They sat around the station stove, ate something from their dinner pails and rested until dawn.

The next morning they put Gus's derailed engine back on the track again, but once more trouble rode with them. About 100 feet down the track there was a sharp curve with a steep bank on the track's lower side. Of course that was the place where the lightweight engine decided to leave the track once more. The rescuers had to work so carefully that it was seven o'clock that night before that stubborn engine was ready to go again. By now the men were sent ahead of the engine to clear the tracks of ice. It was better to be slow and safe.

Now both rescue engines were dangerously low on water and had to go back to Downsville, where there was a water tank. After both engines were filled with water, the men safely made their way back to Shinhopple and on to Centerville, only to find that the derailed freight-train engine waiting there had exhausted its water supply, and the fire had been dumped. What water had been left in this locomotive had been drained to protect the engine boiler from freezing, which would result in some very expensive repairs.

Finally the freight train was raised out of the ditch and onto the track once more. The two live engines pushed the freight train with its dead engine back to East Branch, leaving one of the live engines at East Branch to bring the freight train, which had started on Thursday, out on Monday morning.

The rescue train with the dead engine in tow and a crew of very tired men started back in the direction of Margaretville. It was midnight on Sunday night when they dropped off the local section gang at Shinhopple. It was Monday morning when the exhausted crew got home for some very overdue rest. They had been on duty four days and four nights.

More Derailments

In 1922 a lot of automobile roads were being constructed near Andes, and many gondolas full of sand went over the D&N tracks. The cars would have to be switched at Union Grove from the main line tracks to a crew waiting to take them to Andes.

One day a crew member watching from the station caught sight of the train coming around the bend beyond Union Grove bridge and hollered "here they come," and in the next breath he hollered "there they go." Every one came running to see what he was shouting about.

All they could see was a lot of dust in the air, but knowing their D&N, they knew that the cars of sand were off the tracks and down in the brush.

Another time a load of bulk corn tipped over, tore the roof open, and there was corn all over the nearby countryside.

Cars Off the Tracks at Andes

Andes yard was the scene of many misplaced cars. The feed store and the creamery both had rail sidings of their own. At the feed store the siding was built up to the second story on a trestle, and the creamery siding ran below it at ground level.. Engineers hated to take a chance on an accident when putting their heavy locomotives on this upper trestle. The engineer would boost the car along the track and hope that the brakeman riding on the top of the car would stop it in the right place. Most of the time this worked out just fine. Sometimes the brakeman's timing would be faul-

D&N Engine #1 and a slide near Downsville.
William Capach Collection.

The slide kept coming after the engine stopped.
William Capach Collection.

ty, and then a lot of time and money was spent correcting the mistake. The car had to be placed at the correct doorway or the proper loading platform, or positioned directly over a coal chute that led to storage bins at a lower level. At the feed store a wrong move could leave the car hanging halfway over the end of the trestle or the victim of a steep drop to the creamery track below.

One time the brakeman forgot to couple an air-brake fitting on a car of pea coal for the creamery. The coal-pocket trestle was at the far end of the feed store complex and was used for coal, gravel and sand. He was watching for the exact spot to place the car, motioned the engineer to let go, and turned the brake wheel. The car just kept on going, hit the bumper with such force that it sheared off the track bolts, and the car rode nearly to the ground on the stringers and rails. It didn't damage the car or spill a piece of coal. At that time, all coal gondolas had wood-plank sides. They cut a short piece out of two of the side planks, unloaded the car, and put the car back on the lower tracks. The creamery track had once again proved useful in catching a derailed car from above. One more D&N wreck with a less than tragic ending.

Boxcar in the Delaware River

One time a boxcar derailed at Andes Junction and hung over the edge of a cliff just above the main line track to Shavertown, landing near a large tree known for its strong root system. The workers fastened the block and tackle to this tree stump and applied pressure. The car hadn't even started to move before the tree popped out of the ground, and down went the car, landing on the main line rails first and then tumbling into the Delaware River.

The men used to say that for years afterwards you could feel a slight dip in the track where that boxcar slammed down onto it.

A Load of Coal to the Rescue

There was a very bad snowstorm in the winter of 1921, and the whole region was tied up for several days. There were many deep cuts on the D&N, and these would fill up in a bad storm. As soon as the storm let up, all the section gangs and all the local people that could be hired were set to work (with only shovels) to dig out the tracks. The locomotives could buck some snow with the cowcatchers but would derail in deep snow.

When the railroad filled in the space under Muir's trestle, they used all the dirt from the many cuts on the Andes branch. That left the branch line with very little trouble resulting from mud slides or from large rocks rolling down on the tracks. Sometimes there was trouble with drifting snow, for this part of the railroad was the most mountainous, but there were no deep cuts to become filled with packed snow and ice. Almost everyone burned hard coal in their stoves all winter, and during this bad storm the people in the village of Andes got very low on coal. The local supply ran out.

Just before the storm, a gondola full of coal had been left at Andes Junction, ready to be delivered the next day. The Andes engine crew knew it was there, and the feed store begged them to try to get that car of coal for them. "Nothing ventured, nothing gained," said the crew, and decided to give it a try. To everyone's surprise and relief, the engine was able to push its way through those widened cuts and get the coal.

Note: Before the coming of the railroad, everyone burned wood as fuel; there just wasn't any way to get tons of coal to these rural areas. As soon as coal was cheaply and reliably available, people all took advantage of this improved way to cook and keep warm in the winter. It was rarely possible to keep a wood fire burning all night. You could either get up·several times during the night and replenish the supply of wood in the stove or get up in the morning to a very cold house.

Now the villagers were entirely dependent on the railroad to furnish their fuel in the winter.

The Runaway Passenger Coach

For once here is a story not about something wrong with the D&N, but about another road's coach taking an unauthorized run on D&N tracks. A U&D coach in the Arkville yards lost its air brake pressure and threaded its way through several switches until it was coasting downgrade onto D&N trackage.

The conductor ran after it, piled on board, grabbed the brake wheel, and the brake chain broke. All the conductor could do then was stand on the front of the coach and yell and wave his arms at highway crossings and hope someone could put him on a siding before he ran head-on into something.

He went across the Margaretville highway crossing without encountering anything, but by now he was going about 30 MPH. Down through the Margaretville yards he flew, gaining speed all the time.

Ira Terry heard the rumble coming and rushed out to look. Luckily he had the presence of mind to rush back in and telegraph the station agent at Dunraven to throw the switch for the side track there. There wasn't a minute to lose because the northbound passenger train was due at Dunraven at any minute.

There was more help on the way. John Francisco, a D&N engineer, was waiting on a replacement locomotive for that same northbound passenger train. He jumped off his engine, threw a switch and got the engine out onto the main line, all the while shouting to some other men about what was happening. They all came running out of the shop, and with quick work they had John and his engine through two more switches and onto the main line. Jack Myers jumped onto the pilot to help with the coupler on the front of the rescue engine. About two miles from Dunraven, they were closing in fast, and the conductor on the runaway coach saw what they were trying to do. He ran back and adjusted the knuckle on the coupler of the coach.

Francisco, gaining every second on the runaway coach, finally got near enough to slam hard into the coach. Luckily the couplers locked the first time.

Everyone was very glad that the coach didn't have to take the siding at Dunraven, because there were several boxcars there, but if Francisco hadn't caught it, that would have been the only choice.

This was one time when the D&N was not to blame for anything, but was in fact the rescuing hero. All of the early roads had wrecks and rough times, but sometimes it seemed that the D&N had more than its share.

D&N Engine #5.
William Capach Collection.

D&E wreck at Long Flat on April 1, 1908.
William Capach Collection.

Fighting the snow: NYO&W 4-6-0 camelback locomotive was used to plow the D&N tracks in February, 1920.
John Ham Collection.

The Brill Car had its own plow. Clarence Cowan at East Branch about 1934.
Edward P. Baumgardner Collection.

D&E conductors in new uniforms.
Gus Williams is on the right.

Chapter 6
HUMOR ALONG THE D&N

The Conductor's Cap

Bill Vernold, who lives at East Branch, N.Y., remembers this incident which happened to his father. William Vernold senior was a conductor on the D&N. One day some of the men had a bunch of firecrackers. It was always great fun to see how high something would go with a firecracker under it. Another great joke was to light a firecracker behind some one to see them jump. The railroad gang were always playing jokes on each other, and as soon as one man played a joke on a co-worker, the victim couldn't wait to get even.

Conductor Vernold was proud of his new conductor's hat. Someone decided to see how far this hat would fly with a firecracker under it. The firecracker blew a hole right through the top of the hat. Everyone thought it was great fun to see the cap jump up into the air. Bill also remembers how proud he was one time when he was a boy. His father took Bill along on the train, and when they got to Arkville, his father let Bill "help" turn the locomotive on the turntable — a red letter day for the boy.

The Workers' Diet

The Italian construction workers, who did most of the hard labor building the D&E, bought and cooked their own food. They lived in boxcars or shanties, and most did not speak much English, so dealings with the local population were generally difficult for them. Bill Glendenning lived near one of the work camps, and the workers really liked him. They loved his old white horse, which he had leased to the railroad. The horse was a good, steady worker and saved them a lot of hard labor. To make a change in the Italian workers diet, Bill often sold them woodchuck to cook. That made a little money for Bill and helped to decrease the number of woodchucks on his farm.

One day, as a joke, Bill included a skunk in the supply of woodchucks. Of course the skunk had to be skinned, and the odor got worse and worse, but the man skinning the animal did not give up. When the skunk and woodchucks had all been cut up, they were all tossed into the same pot and cooked. The Italians proclaimed that this did not taste like the cacciatore they had had in their homeland.

Another time the workers wanted to cook some chickens. Bill found an owl which had been caught in a fence, and he included it as just another chicken. As usual, everything landed in the same cook pot. This time the workers told Bill that they didn't want any more of those big-eyed chicks as such food made them all sick.

A Bobcat in the Station

The mountains along the D&N railway were still a little primitive, and many wild animals lived there. Not many of the animals ever came into the villages unless they were being chased by dogs.

In the early days of the railroad Harry Eckert was station agent at Harvard, where the station was across the river from the village. One afternoon, just as he was opening the waiting room door, a bobcat rushed past him, ran through the office, jumped on the telegraph table and crashed through the window without waiting to find an easier way out.

Harry didn't wait to see where the cat went or how much damage was done. He made record time getting to the center of Harvard and seeking the company of several friends. They all went back to the station and made a careful search of the premises, but all they found was a trail of scattered papers and broken glass, showing where the frightened cat had passed through.

The Bag of Chile Tepines

One of the D&N employees came home from a vacation in Arizona with a large bag of nuts that looked like peanuts. There was one big difference between peanuts and the tepines—the tepines were very hot. As the vacationer was telling another employee about the tepines, he had the idea to get together with a few of his co-workers to have some fun.

When the young mail carrier arrived, they offered him some peanuts mixed with tepines. He took a big mouthful and rushed outside to spit them out, but he was good natured about the joke and suggested that they play the same joke on the postal clerk of the Brill Car. The mail carrier's truck was backed up to the railroad tracks with the bag of peanuts and tepines on the tailgate. The Brill postal clerk took a big handful, but on the return trip that day he threw the mailbags out of a half-open door and then slammed the door shut. He would not even speak to anyone at the station.

Not satisfied, the mail carrier took some over to the post office to play the same joke on both the postmaster and his assistant. After several big mouthfuls of water, the assistant asked for some nuts in order to play the same joke on a friend. This time she got even: she made some candy with the nuts and brought it to the post office, treating the mail carrier to candy the next day.

Patching Pants

In general, the workers had a good relationship with the local people; except for the construction crews, most of the employees had lived in the area for a long

The station at Harvard is now a private residence.
M. Twaddell Collection.

time. So when a crew was working between Harvard and East Branch and one of the men tore his pants, the foreman sent him to the neighboring Lotterer farm for repairs.

Mrs. Lotterer was a kind, motherly woman, and she didn't mind helping the man. But she was also a lady, so she sent him to a bedroom to remove his pants and toss them out through a barely-opened door. The repair was made quickly and competently, and the pants were handed back through the crack in the door.

The grateful man tried to pay her, but she was used to doing favors for neighbors and wouldn't accept any money. The worker, slightly flustered by the whole incident, blurted out the usual response to a helpful neighbor: "Thank you very much—I'll do the same for you someday."

The other men found out about the slip of the tongue and teased the man mercilessly. Mel Fingado remembered this story.

Unloading Bagged Lime

Some of the farmers brought a little business to the railroad by ordering lime and fertilizer by the carload. It was much cheaper that way, and sometimes two or more farmers ordered a carload lot together and shared the expense.

One day a carload lot of lime came into Andes, and Art Cross was hired to help unload the car. He was a well-liked farmer and one of the strongest men in the area.

There were a lot of idle men just hanging around the station. They were not interested in helping to unload the car. That was hard work, but they thought they could tease Art into carrying heavier and heavier loads. First one of them asked him why he couldn't carry two bags at once instead of the usual one bag at a time. That would surely get the car unloaded twice as fast. Art carried two bags easily, so the same man teased Art into carrying three bags at once. The man kept on heckling, so Art picked up four bags and deposited them on the man's lap. The man groaned and struggled under this great weight, but no one would help him. Finally he got out from under the bags of lime and left the station. You can bet that he never bothered Art again.

The Railroad Men and the Bull

In October of 1909 a group of trainmen were standing near their engine at the station, watching a herd of cows come across the old covered bridge at Margaretville. The cows had to cross the D&E tracks and head up the highway road toward Arkville. Mixed in among the cows was a Jersey bull, and by the time he had emerged from the bridge, he was very angry. He was not about to follow peacefully along with the cows. He tore down the tracks at full speed, and the engine crew was only about a hundred feet away. As the bull bore down on them, they seemed unable to move and managed to scatter in all directions just in time. Not finding anyone to vent his anger on, he continued at top speed down the track and around a curve. There was another group of men outside the machine shop, and they didn't argue right-of-way with the bull either.

Finally, finding no humans to stand up to him, the bull slowed down and was returned to the herd.

The local newspaper learned of this episode and printed the story. It seemed like everyone in the Delaware Valley knew all about it and the men took a lot of teasing for a few days.

The Customer Was Not Always Right

When the morning passenger train came from Andes, all the passengers with tickets for south of Union Grove had to get off the train and wait for it to go to Arkville and return, before continuing south. Their tickets did not cover the mileage to Arkville and back to Union Grove.

There were many fights between the conductor and the independent local people, but most of it was loud verbal fighting. Sometimes the conductor would get tough and bodily throw one of the more belligerent complainers off the train onto the platform at Union Grove. These country folks loved to "ride the rails," and wanted to have the longest possible ride for their money.

One time a big tough fellow got off at Union Grove and when the conductor yelled "all aboard" he got right back on. The conductor explained the rules, but this fellow informed the conductor that he would go anywhere he wanted to and no one was going to stop him. The conductor considered that he was the master of that rail coach and landed a hard punch on the man's jaw.

The next day the man proved he was a good loser. He held no hard feelings and explained to his friends that the conductor was a better man than he was.

The Frightened Salesman

A flange broke on a boxcar just as the train had cleared Muir's trestle. Most of the cars jumped the track, but none of them tipped over. The passenger car was coupled on behind the boxcars and there were a few passengers. Most of them were local people, and knew all about derailments on the D&N. They all climbed onto the engine and tender, satisfied to get to their destination any way possible.

The locals took it all as part of the ride, but not so a salesman who was aboard. He'd been tossed out of his seat and his sample cases scattered about the floor of the passenger coach. He refused the offered ride on the engine and walked in the direction of Andes, loaded with all his belongings.

He didn't call on his local customers that day and was never seen again at Andes. Folks there said that he hired a horse and carriage to carry him over the hill to his next customer.

Depression Days

Lem Rowland had a sawmill up the Clare and had sold railroad ties to the Delaware & Northern Railroad. The railroad owed Lem $3,500 for the ties, and they were slow in paying for them. James Welch from Margaretville was president of the railroad at this time, and the road was having a lot of trouble trying to pay their bills.

Welch made an appointment with Lem to meet him at the depot and discuss the payment of this outstanding bill. He talked with Lem about hard times and told him that if he'd discount the bill to $2,700, the D&N could pay that much. If not, Welch said the trains would be able to operate only from Downsville to Margaretville and since Lem lived in Corbett that wouldn't please him, would it? Lem said, "Jack's Dam, that would be an awful thing; the railroad is the backbone of the businesses in the valley." Welch kept on hammering at the possibility of the trains running no farther than Downsville. Lem felt awful bad, so Mr. Welch said, "Lem, will you discount your bill?" Lem said, "Mr. Welch, if you've got to have MY MONEY to run your trains, then your engines will NEVER turn a wheel." Carlton O'Connor says that he can still hear Karl Brown laugh as he told him this true story.

Gabe and His Pistol

Sammie Holmes had bid in the job of carrying the mail from the railroad postal car to the post office at Downsville. He had a man working for him who was named Burke Chrisman, but was called Gabe by everyone who knew him. The mail carrier had to carry a gun, but Gabe was afraid of guns, so he took the firing pin out of the pistol. He felt much safer that way, but he was still obeying the law: he was carrying a gun and if anyone tried to hold him up, he couldn't be blamed if he couldn't get the gun out of his pocket. (This was the early 1900s, and the mail robberies of the early rail days were fresh in the memories of government railroad inspectors.)

One day a United States mail inspector came to the station and when Gabe got there the inspector asked to see his gun. Of course Gabe handed it right over, and it didn't take the inspector long to discover that there was no firing pin in the gun. He asked Gabe where it was and Gabe told him that it was in the glove compartment of the mail truck. He made Gabe get it and put it in his gun, and then he ordered Gabe to shoot the gun. Well, Gabe was scared to death. He braced himself on one railroad rail, pointed the gun at a creamery post and pulled the trigger. Karl Brown said the blast sounded like a 16-inch cannon going off. The bullet just floated out of the gun and landed on the opposite side of the railroad track. The pistol had never been cleaned and just wouldn't shoot right. The inspector said, "Burke, I guess you could hit a hold-up bandit if he wasn't more than four feet from you." The inspector said no more. He just walked back to his car and left. He had done what he had been hired to do. This story and the previous one were told by Carlton O'Connor.

The post office at Downsville.
Marjorie Fitch Collection.

Old Ford mail truck meets the Brill Car at Downsville, 1941.
Photo by George Phelps, John Ham Collection.

The Andes station, 1918. Drawing by Harry Archer.

Chapter 7
OTHER HAPPENINGS ALONG THE WAY

A Near Mishap with a Gun

When Ira Terry was working as station agent at Andes, business was good. Sometimes Terry took in as much as $2,000 in a day. He had to take the money home with him at night, as there had been two safe robberies in Andes about that time. Both the feed store and the C. L. Dickson general store had their safes blown open. The railroad insisted that Ira Terry carry a revolver for protection. At night he or his wife hung the gun and gun belt on a hook high above the bed so that their little daughter Marguerite could not reach it.

One morning very early, before her parents woke up, Marguerite somehow climbed over her sleeping mother and father and managed to get the gun. Both parents woke up at the same time and faced the frightening job of getting the gun away from the happy child. She was sitting down between them and waving the loaded gun in the air with happy innocence and did not want to give up her new toy.

Skunk Story

In the summer of 1915, Roma Fitch bid in the job of running the locomotive at Muir's trestle fill site. It was too far to commute from job to home at East Branch, so the railroad officials offered him and another worker a railroad box car to camp out in. Roma and his wife and young daughter and the other family moved in for the summer.

Once in the middle of the night they heard a furtive sound in their cooking pots. Roma quietly lit a lantern, and there stood a skunk. Not finding any open food, the skunk meandered back down the ramp. The next day Roma built a gate to put across the doorway at night.

Tar and Feathers

Divorce was almost unheard of in the early 1900s and if a husband wanted to "play around" he had to be very careful not to let anyone find out about it. Of course the woman was always blamed for the affair, and the husband was the talk of the town for awhile and then he was forgiven. A lady was never supposed to even glance at another woman's husband. Typically the remark about the husband (if he was an important man or well liked) was "well, a man will be a man, you know, and she is a hussy."

In the very early days of the railroad, one of the locomotive engineers became involved with a woman in another town along his route. This went on for quite some time, and maybe he forgot to be quite as discreet as he had been in the beginning. His wife found out about the affair and asked the help of her women

Downsville viewed from Shaw's Hill.
Merlin Twaddell Collection.

friends. They discussed the matter and decided not to confront the husband but to teach that woman of ill repute a good lesson. After all it was really all her fault.

One evening the wife and some of her friends drove to the village where this "other woman" lived. The group proceeded to the woman's home, tore off her clothes, and applied a liberal coat of tar and feathers. Then they escorted her out of town.

The Fox

Schedules on the D&N were not strictly adhered to by the way freight trains. There were many times when the railroaders helped a farmer put out a fire, or rescue a cow or horse that got loose and wandered too near the tracks. The engineers had special whistle signals for the farmers along the line. The whistle signals told the farmer if a special shipment of baby chicks, a valuable baby pig, or anything else needing attention was on board. If his shipment was there, the farmer would rush to the station and pick it up. Otherwise he could just keep on with whatever chores he happened to be doing. This saved the farmer the time that it would take to hitch up the horse and drive to the station just to check on the expected freight.

Railroaders have always been noted for their friendly waves to anyone along the way. One time the Margaretville office got a letter from a jealous farmer near Pepacton, complaining about the freight men waving at his wife. The railroad men had a good laugh over the letter. They didn't wave any more, but they all felt sorry for the lonely woman.

Roma Fitch was engineer on the way freight, and one day he noticed a fox standing down a bank near a brook. He thought it was queer that the fox didn't run from the noise of the engine.

The next day he was almost past the spot before he thought about it. The fox was still there. The third day he remembered it soon enough to slow down as he approached the place. The fox was still there, so Roma stopped the train and climbed down the bank to investigate. The poor fox was caught in a steel trap. It had tried to chew off its own foot to get free. There was a law that if you set a trap, you must visit it once every 24 hours. Obviously this law had been broken.

Since Roma had on heavy overalls and gloves, he was able to get the fox free without any danger of being bitten by the terrified animal. The fox, weakened by its ordeal, seemed to know that the man posed no threat. The only thing that had allowed the poor animal to live that long was the abundance of brook water to drink.

Roma put an old feed sack over its head, then unsprung the trap and carried the fox to the railroad engine. The fox was nearly dead when he got it home, but it seemed to trust its rescuer and allowed its foot to be doctored.

The fox was kept on a dog chain tied near the garage in front of Roma's home, and Roma fed it and gave it water every morning and night. When about two weeks had passed, it seemed well, so one day, after the morning meal, Roma took off the chain and returned the fox to the wild. It happily bounded across the fields and into the woods.

Told by Hannah Malloch Rosenstraus

The railroad company had to dicker with each property owner for right-of-way over their property. Hannah's parents insisted that the railroad build a crossing wherever it was needed in order to get stone and wood out of their property, part of which was on the other side of the tracks. They also insisted that when the railroad was put over their water pipes that extra precautions must be taken not to harm the pipes. She says that her parents probably wouldn't have had water in their house quite so soon if it hadn't been for the railroad. The spring where they got their water was on the other side of the railroad from the house. When the railroad was being built, her folks hurried to dig the ditch and put in the pipes, a job which would be virtually impossible once the tracks had been laid, so they had the water to the house sooner than if the railroad hadn't been built.

Hannah and her folks walked along the railroad track to church on Sunday morning and to services at night. It was a shorter distance, much easier to walk on than the muddy dirt road, and there were no trains on Sundays. Hannah also walked to school at Harvard along the railroad tracks.

The railroad was very important to the farmers, and it was the only means that they had to get their milk to market. There were no snow plows, and sometimes, when the snow was deep, the farmers had to make a path with the horses first before they could get the sleigh or wagon to the train with the milk cans.

They sent their buckwheat and corn to Downsville to be ground into flour or feed for the cattle. Downsville had a water-powered mill, right in town, that used millstones for grinding grains. By changing the stones they could grind the various grains very coarse for cattle and horse feed or fine for home baking needs.

The railroad was the only means the farmers had to get their quarry stone to the important city markets. Cutting stone in the winter when farming work was slower was an important way to add to the farmers' annual income.

On Armistice Day, November 11, 1918, at the end of World War I, the railroad brought an army tank on a flat car to Harvard station. Hannah remembers that the children had a marvelous time climbing all over it.

Downsville when Main Street was a dirt road.
Merlin Twaddell Collection.

Roma Fitch.
Marjorie Fitch Collection.

Chapter 8
TWO DEATHS

Fatal Accident at East Branch

The O&W had sent out an order: If a hotbox was sighted or anything was seen dragging from any of the cars, the station employees should try to catch the eye of someone in the caboose.

The right-of-way through East Branch was straight track, unusual in the winding river valleys of the Catskills. Trains that did not have to stop in East Branch took advantage of this to make up any time lost elsewhere. One day in 1933 a northbound train of empty coal cars was noisily speeding past the station. Witnesses afterward said that the empties made so much noise that one could not hear his companion yelling in his ear.

Arthur Gordon, who was a joint station agent for both the D&N and the O&W, spotted a flaming hotbox on one of the cars, and like the good employee that he was, he tried to get the attention of someone in the caboose. He never noticed that a southbound train was also speeding through East Branch, and he stepped directly in front of the oncoming train.

Mr. Gordon was struck and killed by the southbound freight, right in sight of several of his co-workers. Before the train could be brought to a full stop, it had gone the full length of the 50-car train plus an additional 800 feet.

That was the only time in anyone's memory that two fast trains had been seen passing at East Branch. It was a long time before the local people got over the shock.

Roma Fitch's Fatal Accident

The D&N was a small friendly railroad. Like all other railroads it was a dirty, noisy, hot, and dangerous place to work. You needed to be on your toes at all times. A small slip could mean injury or death. It was the D&N's policy to pay all hospital and doctor bills and full wages to all employees injured in line of duty until they were able to resume work. Unlike most railroads where you only knew a few of your fellow workers, here everyone knew everyone else. It was like having a large family. Usually, all of the workers were willing to help each other any time help was needed.

However, like most families, there were occasions when there were misunderstandings, bickering, and petty jealousies. The railroad era was not the romantic era pictured by most people today. But on no other road were the people of the farms and villages acquainted with and friends with so many railroad workers. There were many tales of workers and non-workers helping each other.

If it hadn't been for one such family, Roma Fitch would have died by himself and not been found until the next day.

Roma was engineer on the Brill Car, which tied up for the night in Downsville. He wouldn't bid in that job until the railroad promised to furnish him a motorized handcar to go between his East Branch home and Downsville daily. They gave him one gas can. When it was empty he would leave it at the shop, and on his return from Arkville he would pick up a full can of fuel. Part of the year it would be dark before he left Downsville for East Branch. There was no fear of meeting any other traffic, as there were no more trains until morning.

One day some school children walking along the tracks near Gregorytown wedged a stone in a switch. It was like putting a penny on the tracks to see what happens; they thought nothing more about it.

When Roma's handcar hit that switch, it left the tracks, turned over, and went down a steep bank. A family living near the tracks had just remarked, "It's about time for Roma to go past." Suddenly they heard a loud noise. Taking a lantern, they went out to investigate. They found him, dragged him up the embankment, and called for help by telephone. They thought he was dead until he groaned.

Dr. Brittain, who lived in Downsville, was the nearest doctor. He came to East Branch every day by train until he thought Roma was out of immediate danger. Roma's wife Julia was a practical nurse, and she nursed him day and night for months.

Finally he was able to get up and walk around. One of his co-workers started the rumor that he was well and able to go to work if he wanted to. Roma was a proud man and decided maybe he could go back to work. He reported for work, and the first day in the yards at Arkville he lost consciousness while driving the Brill Car. As soon as his foot was off the pedal, the car slowed and drifted at about 5 MPH. It came to a stop when it collided with a U&D locomotive. There was $8,000 worth of damage to the Brill Car but none to the locomotive. That was on September 16, 1932, and after months of pain, in bed most of the time, Roma Fitch died March 12, 1933.

After his death the railroad denied any responsibility and refused to pay any compensation to his widow. They claimed (despite the fact that no one but Roma had used the handcar for years, and the railroad had always furnished the gas) that they did not know he was using the handcar.

Railroading was hard on the Fitch family. First Roma's brother Morris was killed on the Lehigh Valley in 1918, then another brother, Aubrey, also on the Lehigh Valley, in 1928. Roma died of injuries in 1933, and his brother Jason died on the Lehigh Valley in 1943.

The O&W double track at East Branch where Arthur Gordon was killed. D&N train with Engine #5 is ready to leave. William Capach Collection.

Dr. Robert Brittain of Downsville, official D&N physician. As a young doctor
he rode a horse and carried his medical supplies in saddlebags. Later he used
a horse and buggy and, eventually, a Model T Ford.
Evelyn Murtagh Collection.

Engine #3 at East Branch in 1915. Roma Fitch, left, and his brother-in-
law, Charles Scott (not a railroad employee).
Marjorie Fitch Collection.

Riverside Farm at Arena took in summer boarders.
Merlin Twaddell Collection.

Chapter 9
EFFECTS OF THE RAILROAD

Fringe Benefits

The D&N was a small railroad, and the management understood that their employees were not making much money, so they tried to help them in any other way that they could. When Roma Fitch said he would like to bid on the Muir's trestle job, the railroad offered to make a boxcar available for him and another family to camp out in for the summer. When a conductor wanted to bid on a job out of Andes, but lived too far to commute every night, they offered him an unused caboose to stay in.

There was a lot of fertile land on the wye at East Branch that was not being used for anything. Roma Fitch asked permission to plant a garden on this land. Permission was gladly given. He planted a large garden every year for many years and never lost any produce to theft or vandalism.

Some employees were allowed to take as many bags of soft coal home as they needed to keep warm in winter. They were to put the number of bags that they used each month on their monthly time sheets. Probably others, not connected with the railroad, burned soft coal in the winter, too.

When the road replaced the ties, the section men were told to pile the old ties along the tracks instead of throwing them over the bank. That way the employees could take home the old ties and saw them up in lengths suitable for use in their stoves. After splitting the ties with an ax the men had enough wood for the whole winter. The ties were full of cinders, and once in awhile a spike would be overlooked. This made it very hard on the saw blades. Also between the soot from the soft coal (which burned dirtier than hard coal) and the creosote from the old ties, the chimneys had to be cleaned quite often. If this was neglected, you would have a chimney fire.

One time an employee wanted to build a wood shed in his back yard. He knew that, near his home, a boxcar had gone over the bank toward the river. There was a lot of useable lumber just going to waste. The railroad had already salvaged the trucks and other metal parts, so there was nothing left worth the time and effort it would take to haul the car up the bank. However, the employee could float the lumber across the Delaware and get it home by pick-up truck. He asked permission to do this. The D&N was glad to get rid of the rest of the wreck. The employee built his shed entirely from this lumber and used the boxcar doors as a lean-to for one side of the building.

This little road never had much money to work with but always helped in any other way possible. Such consideration produced intense loyalty among the employees of the D&N. I don't believe there were many employees who didn't put in a lot of extra hours every week that were never reported. If they saw anything that needed to be done, they did it without talking about it afterwards.

Effect of the Railroad on the Local People

There is one effect this railroad had on the local population that was praised by families all up and down the Delaware Valley. Before the coming of the "iron horse," it was a long and difficult journey to go even 10 miles from home. Now with the railroad carrying both mail and passengers, it was easy to communicate with loved ones.

A mother could send a letter (in this area even most of the girls could read and write) to announce that she and all the kids were coming for a visit on a certain day and train, and be confident that a horse and buggy would be waiting at the station at the appointed time. Sometimes it was just so wonderful to be able to go shopping at a store in one of the towns. That was a real luxury for these stay-at-home families. The schedule of the railroad made it possible to go shopping and return the same day. Now, while riding on the train, people had someone different to talk to and a chance to exchange ideas and information.

Since this was a farming area there was always lots of food when extra folks dropped in. The men opened up that hidden bottle of apple jack while doing chores in the barn, and the ladies gossiped in the kitchen while preparing food. There was never time to sit in the parlor. That was reserved for weddings, funerals or a visit from the preacher.

Right from the beginning of the road they recorded 140,000 paying passengers per year, and this was almost all local people. Of course there were also non-paying passengers who didn't show up in the figures. Workers' families rode free, and so did many of the poorer local people who happened to know the conductor.

Searing had planned to make the Delaware Valley a summer vacation land. Although a few farms had some summer boarders, these plans and hopes never materialized. However the D&N and the O&W did sponsor joint excursion rates to New York City. The cost was $5.15 from Arkville and $4.60 from Downsville. Many farm folks went to the "big city" for the first time. This would have been beyond their wildest dreams before the railroad. It cost 10 cents to ride from Corbett to East Branch. These people decided that it was "great sport to ride the cars" and

did so every chance they had. The 10 cents was not always easy to come by in those days.

At one time the D&N printed 500-mile reduced-fare ticket booklets, perforated in one-mile units. For example: If you traveled four miles, you used four tickets. School pupils who rode the train to school were also given reduced fare tickets. All employees could get a pass for themselves and their families to travel not only on the D&N but also on the two connecting railroads. Being able to travel on both the Ulster & Delaware and the Ontario & Western railroads expanded their traveling plans. They had free transportation to New York City, and could send their children to a local high school—an opportunity they themselves had never had. By meeting different people they expanded their knowledge beyond their own communities.

In some of the early villages, the railroad had the only telephone in town. In case of an emergency, anyone was allowed to use this telephone. Many a call to a local doctor was made from the railroad phone. Doctor Brittain at Downsville would always respond to a call. After giving advice on the phone, he drove a horse and buggy to the home and would stay as long as necessary.

The railroad made it much easier to vote on election day. The local people could ride the mail train to the nearest polling places. After voting, they would visit with friends until the returning train came through. Then they went back to their homes after a pleasant outing. That was much easier than hitching up the horse and wagon. Of course until the passage of the 19th Amendment only the men could vote. After the amendment, it took a few years before most of the women felt comfortable in the voting booth.

On November 2, 1915, Delaware County was voted dry and Woman's Suffrage was voted down. In 1924 about 80 voters rode the train to Colchester and voted to form their own school district.

These people, who had been isolated for so many generations, were finally set free.

Epilogue

This little railroad, which lasted a relatively short time (1905-1942), brought so much good to this part of Delaware County. It pushed the area into the twentieth century ahead of some other sections of the country. Until the dirt roads were changed by some kind of hard top, they were almost unuseable every spring and for most of the winter. When the first automobiles appeared, many people put them in the barn, up on blocks, for the winter. The macadam roads changed all that, and soon the little "Tin Lizzie" grew until big trucks appeared that could rival the railroads.

It is too bad that the people's loyalty moved so quickly from the railroad to the new trucks. The trucks were better for lots of jobs, such as delivering small loads directly to your door. But the railroads could haul very heavy loads (coal, feed, heavy machinery) much more efficiently and cheaply. Think how much longer our highways would last without heavy truck traffic. Both trucks and railroads have their own place, where each one does certain jobs best.

There is now very little left on the East Branch of the Delaware River to show that there was ever a railroad there. The station at East Branch burned to the ground in the summer of 1988.

In a few places the old right-of-way is used as a county road. No one unfamiliar with the area would ever recognize these roads as a once busy railway. There are very few persons left who ever worked on the D&N, but it is still fondly remembered in the region it served, and it is hoped there that it will never be completely forgotten.

When Frederick Searing first saw the area there were a few signs that someone had done a little grading and filling in preparation for building a railroad. Now there are a few places where one can still see a little grading and filling—all that is left of the beloved line called the Delaware & Northern Railroad.

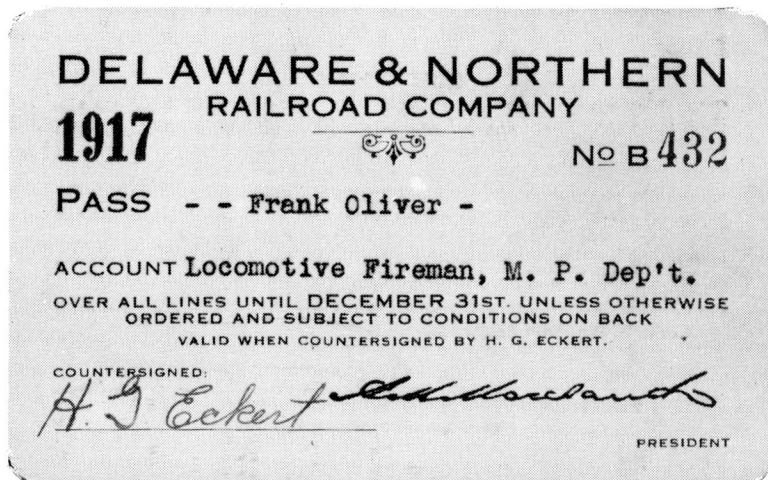

Collection of Edward P. Baumgardner.

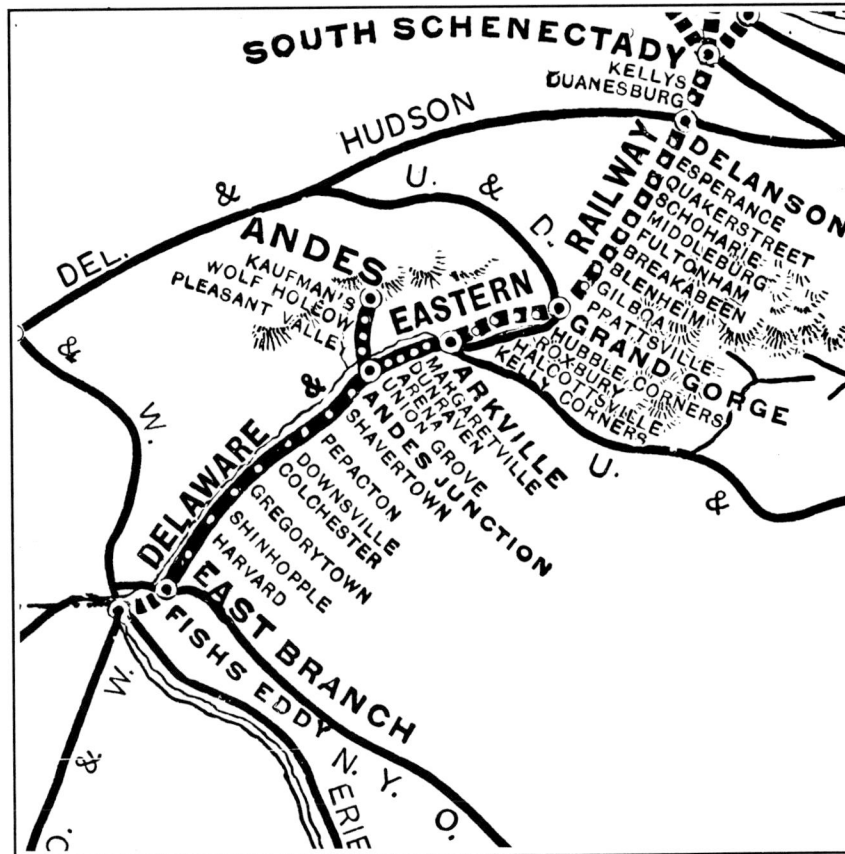

The D&N served four townships in Delaware County, New York: Hancock, Colchester, Andes, and Middletown. This map shows all of the communities on the line, as well as those on the proposed D&E extension north from Arkville.

Detail of a map from the collection of Edward P. Baumgardner.

Chapter 10
THE TOWNS IT SERVED
An Album of Post Card Views

Introduction by Stanley Horton

The communities served by the D&N were all small, and none had any large industries. We will start our tour of the road from the south end at East Branch, where the Delaware & Northern met the New York, Ontario & Western and travel northeast to Arkville, where the D&N met the Ulster & Delaware.

At East Branch the D&N shared the O&W depot and agent, and there they had a wye and a small yard, and a coal dump to fuel the locomotives. The night watchman would shovel coal from where it had been dumped on the ground into the tender.

From the end of the wye the railroad crossed the Beaver Kill and old Route 17 and started up along the east bank of the Delaware River. There was a small sawmill along the river, and the D&N had a water tank about a mile from town, but in later years the railroad got their water from the O&W spout in East Branch.

The next place up the pike was Centerville, where in the early days an acid factory was located across the river from the tracks. A swing bridge was constructed to get the products from the factory to the railroad. Centerville had no depot.

About a mile and a half above Centerville was the hamlet of Harvard. The tracks were across the river and higher than the main part of town, and a small station and a coal and feed dump were located here. A highway bridge crossed the river to the town and to

the acid factory, which was located a short distance up Baxter Brook.

The next hamlet was Shinhopple, which also had a small acid factory across the river and up Trout Brook. The railroad had a station at Shinhopple with a passing track and a stone dock.

The next place was one that the railroad could say they made possible. After the railroad came through, the firm of Corbett and Stuart built a large acid factory, sawmill, and workers' quarters at a place called Campbell's Flats. They named their company town Corbett. Until it closed in 1934, the acid factory was one of the road's biggest shippers and one of the few originating freight points on the D&N.

Three miles above Corbett was Downsville, where once again the railroad was on the wrong side of the river. Downsville was reached via a covered bridge that is still in use. A large station, a creamery and a three-track yard were at Downsville and also a water tank.

From Downsville to Margaretville the old right-of-way is now under water. The Pepacton Dam, finished in the early 1950s to impound a water supply for the city of New York, saw to that. The places once served by the D&N, and now under water, were Pepacton, Shavertown, Andes Junction, Union Grove, Arena and Dunraven. On the Andes branch were Pleasant Valley, Wolf Hollow, Kaufman's and the village of Andes.

East Branch from the hill above.
Merlin Twaddell Collection.

Bridges at East Branch: the railroad bridge over the Beaver Kill and the highway bridge (New York State Route 17) over the Delaware River.
Marjorie Fitch Collection.

Main Street, Harvard.
Marjorie Fitch Collection.

School house and Methodist Church at Harvard.
Marjorie Fitch Collection.

Malloch farm buildings along the railroad tracks between East Branch and Harvard.
Ada Marie Prill Collection.

Old House Eddy on the Delaware.

**Old House Eddy near Shinhopple. At one time, great timber rafts were
floated down the river. Rafters gave names to the eddies.**
Merlin Twaddell Collection.

Trout Brook near Shinhopple.
Merlin Twaddell Collection.

Delaware River near Shinhopple. Route 30 is on the left.
Marjorie Fitch Collection.

Covered bridge at Colchester. It was said to be the longest covered bridge across the Delaware River.
William Capach Collection.

The Downsville stage provided transportation along the East Branch of the Delaware before the coming of the D&E. The railroad era brought an end to the legendary exploits of stage drivers like folk hero Cage Corbin.
Merlin Twaddell Collection.

**The Hulbert-Holmes Concrete Block in Downsville housed the National Bank, a
drug store, and in the back, an opera house (later a movie theater).**
Merlin Twaddell Collection.

Downs House & Opera House, DOWNSVILLE, N. Y.

Downs House, Downsville.
Merlin Twaddell Collection.

The Hulbert Block at Downsville — a popular shopping place.
Merlin Twaddell Collection.

Holmes Dam furnished power for a grist mill at Downsville.
Marjorie Fitch Collection.

The Downsville Concert Band furnished music for the opening ceremonies of the D&E on November 17, 1906.

Merlin Twaddell Collection.

J. E. Goodsir General Merchandise, Main Street, Pepacton.

Bernard Wadler Collection.

Pepacton and the East Branch Valley.
Bernard Wadler Collection.

The covered bridge at Pepacton.
William Capach Collection.

Pepacton, February 20, 1920.
William Capach Collection.

Pepacton Station.
Merlin Twaddell Collection.

View of Shavertown.
William Capach Collection.

Shavertown with D&N tracks in the foreground.
Merlin Twaddell Collection.

Shavertown post office.
Marjorie Fitch Collection.

Wintertime at the Shavertown station.
William Capach Collection.

This card is captioned: "Where the Good Roads meet at Andes, N.Y."
The road to left leads down the Tremper Kill to the present Shavertown bridge
across the Pepacton Reservoir; to the right, over Cabin Hill to De Lancey.
Bernard Wadler Collection.

View of Andes.
Bernard Wadler Collection.

Andes High School.
Merlin Twaddell Collection.

Station at Andes. Perhaps the construction materials piled there are bound for the Gerry estate.
William Capach Collection.

D&N bridge at Union Grove.
Bernard Wadler Collection.

Jenkin's Falls, Union Grove.
Bernard Wadler Collection.

Main Street, Union Grove.
Merlin Twaddell Collection.

The bridge at Mill and Main Streets in Union Grove.
Merlin Twaddell Collection.

Bird's eye view of Arena.
Merlin Twaddell Collection.

The post office on Maple Avenue, Arena.
Bernard Wadler Collection.

The valley of the East Branch of the Delaware River from Perch Lake Hill near Arena.
Marjorie Fitch Collecton.

Lower Main Street, Arena.
Merlin Twaddell Collection.

Main Street, Margaretville.
Bernard Wadler Collection.

Masonic Temple, Margaretville.
Bernard Wadler Collection.

Pocantico Inn, Main Street, Margaretville. The movie crew for The Single Track stayed here in 1920. The movie was filmed on the Andes branch of the D&N.
Bernard Wadler Collection.

Main Street, Margaretville.
Collection Bernard Wadler.

Looking East, Arkville, N. Y., Catskill Mountains

Arkville.
Merlin Twaddell Collection.

Part of Arkville Village, Arkville, N. Y., Catskill Mountains.

Arkville, D&N station is on the left.
Merlin Twaddell Collection.

Schoolhouse, Arkville
Marjorie Fitch Collection.

Covered Bridge, Arkville
Merlin Twaddell Collection.

D&N heavy brass switch lock with keys.
Ada Marie Prill Collection.

Appendix
RECORDS OF THE D&E AND D&N

Officers, Employees, Equipment, etc.

Equipment of the Delaware & Eastern on June 30, 1906

3 coaches, 2 combines
1 express, mail, and baggage
8 milk cars, 20 boxcars, 40 flatcars,
1 caboose, 4 D&E engines

Locomotives of the Delaware & Eastern

No.	Name of Locomotive	Type	Builder	Year Built	Year Scrapped
1	F. F. Searing	4-4-0	Cooke	1884	1929
2	R. B. Williams	4-4-0	Dickson	1884	1922
3	A. C. Fairchild	2-6-0	Dickson	1881	1911
4	H. M. George	4-4-0	Dickson	1884	1930
5	Russell Murray	4-4-0	Dickson	1882	1912

All of these engines were formerly owned by the Delaware, Lackawanna & Western and sold to the D&E, used. Engine #3 cost $4,400. Engines #1, #2, #3 and #4 were purchased in 1905, and #5 was purchased in 1908. All engines had canvas wind curtains between the cab and the tender to make it a little more comfortable in winter.

In the early life of the road the locomotives had been equipped with special cowcatchers to fend off snow, rocks, mud and boulders. They helped to avoid a little trouble if there wasn't too much on the rails.

All locomotives were given names as long as Searing controlled the road.

Specifications of Locomotives of the Delaware & Eastern

No.	Type	Cylinders	Drivers	Weight Total	Builder	Date
1	4-4-0	19"x 24"	68"	94,000	Cooke	1884
2	4-4-0	19"x 24"	62"	98,000	Dickson	1884
3	2-6-0	18"x 24"	57"	97,572	Dickson	1881
4	4-4-0	19"x 24"	62"	98,000	Dickson	1884
5	4-4-0	19"x 24"	56.5"	92,100	Dickson	1882

Specifications of Locomotives of the Delaware & Northern

No.	Type	Builder	Year Built	Purchased	Scrapped
1	4-4-0	Baldwin	1902	1911	1933
2	4-4-0	Baldwin	1902	1911	1933
3	4-4-0	Baldwin	1902	1911	1944
4	4-4-0	Dickson (ex-D&E #2)	1884	1905	1921/29
5	4-4-0	Cooke (ex-D&E #1)	1884	1905	1921/29
6	4-4-0	Dickson (ex-D&E #4)	1884	1905	1921/29
7	4-6-0	Brooks	1900	1923	1929/42
10	2-6-0	Lima	1910	1929	1944
10	Motor	Brill	1926	1926	after 1942

Engines #1, #2 and #3, formerly owned by the South Indiana Railroad, had all sat out in the weather for a number of years. They were reshopped by Baldwin in 1911 before delivery to the D&N. Engine #2 was scrapped in 1933. It ran into some ice and the lead truck got cockeyed and came off. The engine ran over the pilot truck and cracked one of the cylinders. Art Barringer was the engineer.

Engine #10 was an ex-Emporia Manufacturing Co., purchased from Birmingham Rail & Locomotive Co. Engine #7 was a compound, and had the valve gear changed to simple before the D&N purchased it. It never worked right after the change. It was ex-Buffalo, Rochester & Pittsburgh #186. The three Baldwins and #7 were purchased from Southern Iron & Equipment Co. Roma Fitch said that #7 couldn't pull a flea off a dog.

The Brill Car was powered by a 250 HP, 6-cylinder Winton gasoline engine with five speeds ahead and five in reverse. It was front-wheel drive and was 65 feet long. It could carry 29 passengers and was in service at the closing of the road.

Locomotives #3 and #10 were in service at the closing of the road.

Names Used by This Railroad

Names Used by This Railroad	Year	Remarks
Delaware & Eastern Railroad	1905-1907	Searing control
Delaware & Eastern Railway	1907-1911	Searing control
Delaware & Northern Railroad	1911-1921	1st. Receivership
Delaware & Northern Receivership	1921-1928	2nd. Receivership
Delaware & Northern Railway	1929-1942	Sam Rosoff, owner

Delaware & Northern Rolling Stock

Passenger Cars

No.	Type	Length	Capacity	Remarks
1-5	Passenger	55 ft.	60	Open platform, wood, used 1906
50-54	Passenger/baggage	54 ft.	28	Open platform, wood, used 1906

The seats, backs and armrests in the passenger-coach sections were all made of red plush.

Freight Cars

No.	Type	Length	Capacity	Remarks
101-108	Milk	52 ft.	—	Wood, #108 wrecked 1908, rest sold in 1920
501-557	Box	40 ft.	30 T	Wood, 47 cars sold 1912-1916
1001-1110	Flat	40 ft.	30 T	Wood, 65 cars sold 1911-1918
A, C, Z	Caboose			Cars C and Z sold by 1918
MWA	Derrick and Tool Car			Steel frame
MWT	Tool and Outfit Car			Rebuilt old box car

The railroad bought much more freight rolling-stock than they needed. Perhaps they were looking forward to the coal line that they hoped to build.

Officers at Delaware & Eastern Headquarters, 7 Wall Street, New York City

Frederick F. Searing	President
Alfred C. Fairchild	1st Vice President
Russell Murray	2nd Vice President
Harry M. George	Secretary-Treasurer
R. B. Williams	General Manager
Otto F. Wagenhorst	Chief Engineer
Edward J. Welch	General Counsel
F. P. Lincoln	Charge of Construction

Operating Office at Margaretville, September 1905

R. B. Williams	Superintendent and General Manager
John J. Conway	Chief Clerk
James J. Welch	Train Dispatcher
Otto F. Wagenhorst	Chief Engineer
E. Payson Cooke	Andes General Passenger Agent
F. P. Lincoln	Construction

Some Financial Backers in 1905

Col. William Barber	Hanover Bank, N. Y. C.
Joseph J. Jermyn	Coal holdings
John W. Griggs	Pittsburgh, Pa.
Andrew M. Moreland	Pittsburgh, Pa.
Frederick F. Searing	Searing and Co., N. Y. C.

Officers of the Delaware & Northern in 1913

Andrew Moreland, Pittsburgh, Pa.	President
William H. Seif, Pittsburgh, Pa.	1st Vice President
Joseph J. Jermyn, Scranton, Pa.	2nd Vice President
Howard Feist, Pittsburgh, Pa	Secretary/Treasurer

These men all had financial interest in the road.

Operating Office at Margaretville in 1913

James J. Welch	Superintendent
Harry Eckert	Chief Clerk
Robert Young	Head Bookkeeper
Andrew C. Benjamin	Traffic Accountant
George Denton	Auditor
Harry D. Miller	General Freight and Passenger Agent
David P. Dickson	Stenographer and Clerk
Ira E. Terry	Freight Agent and Assistant Dispatcher
Jacob Creveling	Maintenance of Way
John Funari	Mail and Baggage

Delaware & Northern Railway Office Force on October 17, 1942

Samuel R. Rosoff	President
James J. Welch	Vice President, Superintendent, Freight and Passenger Agent
Ira E. Terry	Chief Clerk, Assistant to Vice President, Chief Dispatcher and Purchasing Agent
Harry G. Eckert	Assistant Secretary and Treasurer, Head Bookkeeper, and Assistant Dispatcher
Charles A. Snyder	Traffic Accountant Dispatcher

Clerks and Stenographers Employed at Various Times

Evelyn Becker
David Dickson
Florence Kelly Eckert
Glenford Faulkner
Constance Teed Hagerty
Sylvanus Kelly
Lawrence Larson

Miss McCann
Joseph McKiernan
Harvey O'Kelly
Robert Stuart
James A. Walsh
Vivian Terry Winner

Engineers and Firemen
(Some Started as Hostlers and Were Promoted to Firemen and Then to Engineers)

Leo Ackerly
Arthur Barringer
Art Bullis
Clarence Cowan
Horton Decker
Reynolds Decker
Harry Funari
Horton Funari
Roma Fitch
John Francisco
Willam Hubbard
Abram Jones
F. W. Major
O. B. (Barney) Marks
Dan McCann

Harvey McCumber
Calvin Miller
Earl Monroe
Frank Oliver
W. A. Pattberg
I. N. (Pop) Philips
Joseph Rider
Harry Rukgaber
George Sliter*
Laurie Sliter*
William Sliter*
Edward H. Smith
O. K. Smith
Eno (Bill) Strong
Ed Yaple

*This is the way this name appears in Archer's book. Roma Fitch pronounced it "Slater."

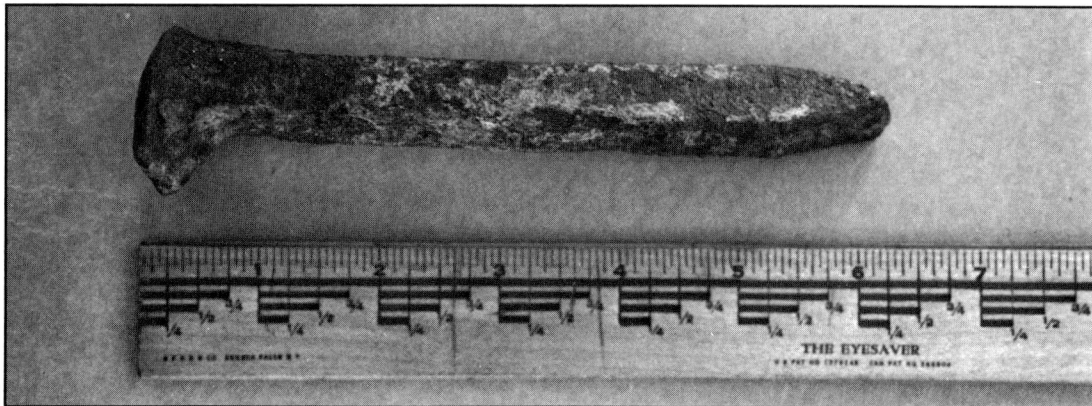

Spike from D&N tracks.
Ada Marie Prill Collection.

Conductors and Trainmen

E. D. Avery	Howard Gavett	Ernest Sheable
Floyd Barber	William B. Germond	Millard Simonson
Ernest Barnhart	Howard (Pete) Gill	Frank Smith
Floyd Bennett	J. G. Harris	Charles M. Spiers
Horace Brannon	Fred Horton	B. Sulliger
Earl Brown	Lavern Hunt	Harry Terry
William D. Brown	A. Jones	Robert C. Terry
Charles H. Burdick	Martin Kneewasher	Berton Todd
John Burnside	Howard Liddle	J. Tompkins
Thomas Chamberlain	Winfred Liddle	Seymour Tompkins
Frank Cole	Charles Martin	Andrew Van Bumble
Emmett Eckert	Charles Monahan	Irving Van Valkenberg
Walt Edwards	Charles Oliver	William Vernold
Marshall Emerson	LeRoy Place	Harvey Wickham
A. O. Finch	Raymond Place Jr.	Walter Wickham
Aubrey Fitch	Carl Rider	Augustus Williams
Morris Fitch	Earl Rider	Chauncy Winnie
Samuel Fullerton	Joseph Rider	Henry Winnie
Arthur Gavett	Lewis E. Sanford	John A. Young

Engineer Dan McCann and conductor Sam Fullerton came from Georgia and worked on the D&N. Nothing more is known of McCann, but Fullerton worked on the road for decades.

Express Messengers

Ralph Fitzgerald	John Fowler	Elliott Gladstone
Frank Haner	Jacob Kortright	Charles Van Hosen

D&N monthly school ticket issued in June, 1935.

School ticket: Edward P. Baumgardner Collection. All others on following pages: John Ham Collection.

Station Agents and Telegraphers About 1912

Fred W. Bishop	Arkville, N. Y. (Joint agent for U&D.)
Daniel L. Todd	Margaretville, N. Y.
George E. Gladstone	Dunraven, N. Y.
Elmer A. Seeley	Arena, N. Y.
Harry R. Prindle	Union Grove, N. Y.
LeRoy Jenkins	Andes, N. Y.
Ira Terry	Andes, N. Y.
H. W. (Biddy) Doyle	Shavertown, N. Y.
Willis A. Terry	Pepacton, N. Y.
Arthur H. Carman	Downsville, N. Y.
Raymond L. Steenrod	Shinhopple, N. Y.
William M. Hardenburgh	Harvard, N. Y.
Jack Cassidy	East Branch, N. Y. (Joint agent for O&W.)

Note: All except Mr. Gladstone were also telegraphers. Mrs. Carmen assisted her husband at Downsville. Mrs. Pearl Jenkins assisted her husband at Andes (she was also a telegrapher). Mrs. Martha Terry assisted her husband at Andes, when Ira Terry relieved Mr. Jenkins at Andes.

Carlton O'Connor says that station agent Hardenburgh had only one hand as the result of an accident that blew off one hand. The accident happened in a stone quarry up by the Purdy farm at the junction of Gregory and Telford Hollows. When he applied for a job at Margaretville, they were quite skeptical about hiring him. They decided to take him on for the "easy" job of station agent at the sleepy village of Harvard, and he held the position for many years. He was very strong and could toss a heavy trunk into the express car. It only took one hand to operate a telegraph key, and he was a very good telegrapher.

Section Foremen About 1912

Wm. H. Stevens	General Track Supervisor
Pasco Dillello	Secured Employment for immigrants
Frank Paden	Foreman at Margaretville, N. Y.
James Francisco	Foreman at Union Grove, N. Y.
Harvey Winne	Foreman at Shavertown, N. Y.
W. H. Spoor	Foreman at Pepacton, N. Y.
Allie Miller	Foreman at Downsville, N. Y.
Bert Daugherty	Foreman at Shinhopple, N. Y.
Samuel Lewis	Foreman at East Branch, N. Y.
Angelo Lodovice	Foreman at Andes, N. Y.

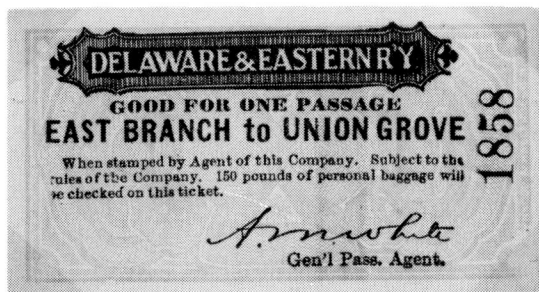

DELAWARE & EASTERN R'Y
GOOD FOR ONE PASSAGE
EAST BRANCH to UNION GROVE 1858
When stamped by Agent of this Company. Subject to the rules of the Company. 150 pounds of personal baggage will be checked on this ticket.
Gen'l Pass. Agent.

DELAWARE & NORTHERN R. R.
NOT TRANSFERABLE
Good only for One Continuous Passage
EAST BRANCH COLCHESTER
To be begun on the day of sale as indicated by stamp of authorized Agent on back hereof, or before midnight of the following day. Liability for baggage is limited to $150, unless greater value is stated, and payment made therefor at time of checking.
Gen'l Pass. Agent.

Other Section Foremen or Men in Track Service at Various Times

Harrison Barber
Bennie Cicio
Tony Cicio
Dewitt Day (steam shovel)
John Fluckiger
David Fuhry

Leon Furch (steam shovel)
Floyd Hawkins
Guido (Squeak) Lodovice
Fred S. Myers
Mike Lodovice
Fred Ziegler

Note: In the early days of the railroad, there were nine section-gangs consisting of one foreman and six to eight laborers. Toward the end of the road, they had four section-gangs consisting of one foreman and one laborer.

The handcars that the section crews used were hand-pump cars, and if the grade was too steep, at least one man would get off and push. These cars could really roll, but they weren't much on a grade.

Mechanical Department About 1912

Lester DePuy	Master Mechanic
George (Jack) Myers	Shop Foreman
Charles A. Boyd	Boilermaker
Milton Mills	Boilermaker's Helper
Grover Henderson	Machinist
Jack (Jersey) Gulnick	Blacksmith
George McCumber	Machinist and Stone Mason
Vet Walley	Blacksmith
Brink Knickerbocker	Carpenter and Car Builder
William H. Decker	Carpenter
Frank Meade	Carpenter and Concrete Builder
M. Lee DePuy	Machinist
George Balcom	Stationary Boiler Fireman
William (Wild Bill) Decker	Engine Hostler
Horton Decker	Engine Hostler
John Hewitt	Helper
Frank Kelley	Machinist
Humphrey Jones	Boilermaker's Assistant and Machinist
Raymond Place	Stone Mason and Helper
G. C. Squires	Car Repairman
Byron Sheppard	Engine Hostler and Fireman
Charles Bently	Shop Clerk, Telegrapher, Storekeeper

Others Employed in the Mechanical Department at Various Times

Earl Balcome	Grover Henderson	Ed Myers
John T. Baxter	Howard Henderson	Lynn Neidig
L. D. Bishop	James Hendricks	David Nichols
Conrad Bloom	John Hinckley	Miles O'Riley
Mike Cerquozzi	Marshall Hughes	Joseph Pedulla
Everett Edmonds	Charles Hunter	Roy Reichard
Charles Fairbairn	Embree Johnson	Chet Scofield
Earl Fairbairn	Douglas Kelly	W. H. Sliter
Earl Fisk	Edward Kittle	Alfred Stewart
Edward Funari	Burdett Mason	Austin Stewart
Howard Gavette	Ralph Mead	Warner Teed
Frank Grisola	Nelson Mott	Charles Winnie
Bill Gulnick	Andrew Myers	Russell Winnie
Denzil Haight		

Mail, Express and Baggage Handlers

Edward Funari	Embree Johnson	Harry Odell
John Funari	Ransom Ives	Paul Van Hosen
Walter Wickham	Raymond Winner	

Other People Employed at Various Times for Various Jobs

Ordway Atkin	Pearl Jenkins	Charles Reyen
A. S. Banker	James Joyce	Norman Rickard
W. C. Bentley	Harry Keator	Daniel Sickler
Karl Brown	Volney Keator	Charles Snyder
John Dutcher	Earl Krum	Claude Tiffany
Harry B. Eckler	Peter Leming	Harrison Todd
Harry Ennist	Fred Lewis	F. J. Verdon
M. J. Faulkner	Elmer McMichaels	L. R. Vin Arx
Fred Fitzgibbons	Fred McMorris	Lewis C. Wheat
Arthur Gladstone	Thomas Myers	Vere L. White
Arthur Gordon	R. G. Neidig	Ray E. Woodin
Grover Hedges	Floyd Osborne	

Note: Arthur Gordon and Fred McMorris were both station agents at East Branch. They served for both the Delaware & Northern and the New York, Ontario & Western railroads.

Abbreviations Used for Railroad Names

D&E	Delaware & Eastern
D&N	Delaware & Northern
D&H	Delaware & Hudson
NYO&W	New York, Ontario & Western
O&W	New York, Ontario & Western
U&D	Ulster & Delaware

Pupils in Wreck of September 5, 1934

The names of the 14 pupils involved in the wreck of the Brill Car are as follows:

Glenford Close	Madeline Fuller	Edna Moore
Nellie Close	Olive Greene	Artis Rickard
Alba Dodaro	Sarah Greene	Russell Seeley
Virginia Dodaro	George Gregory	Mabel VanKeuren
Leroy Fairbairn	James Martin	

Accident Record of the Brill Car

The crew of the Brill Car kept a record of everything hit by the car, of every time it was ditched and the name of the engineer at the time of the accident.

	Autos	Cows	Ditched	Locomotive
Cowan	4	1	4	
Fitch	2			1
Rider	1		1	

Tearing up the rails on the D&N during the summer of 1943. This is Shavertown and the partly dismantled building is the D&E creamery.

Photo by Darrell S. Atkin, Edward P. Baumgardner Collection.

FOR FURTHER READING

Harry D. Archer, *The Damn Nuisance: Story of the Delaware & Northern Railway 1905 to 1942* no date [1971], no place of publication

Gerald M. Best, *The Ulster and Delaware: Railroad Through the Catskills*, San Marino, CA, 1972

Alf Evers, *The Catskills: From Wilderness to Woodstock*, New York, 1972

Douglas De Natale, *Two Stones for Every Dirt: The Story of Delaware County, New York*, Fleischmanns, NY, 1987

William H. Helmer, *O&W: The Long Life and Slow Death of the New York, Ontario and Western Railway*, Berkeley, 1959.

Alice H. Jacobson, *Beneath Pepacton Waters*, Andes, NY, 1988

Frank Daniel Myers III, *The Wood Chemical Industry in the Delaware Valley*, Middletown, NY, 1986

Manville B. Wakefield, *To the Mountains by Rail*, Grahamsville, NY, 1970

Ghost train in the Catskills.
Drawing by Harry Archer depicts the ghost of a D&N train between Union Grove
and Shavertown, both buried beneath New York City's Pepacton Reservoir.